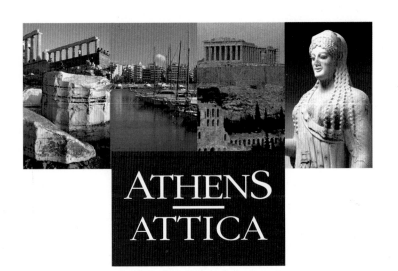

ATHENS
ATTICA

GREECE

MINISTRY OF TOURISM
GREEK NATIONAL TOURISM ORGANISATION

1. A section of the pediment of the Athens Academy building.

Athens is the historical capital of Europe. Athens has a long history, dating from the first settlement in the Neolithic age. In the 5th Century BC (the "Golden Age of Pericles") – the culmination of Athens' long, fascinating history – the city's values and civilisation acquired a universal significance. Political thought, theatre, the arts, philosophy, science, architecture, among other forms of intellectual thought, reached an epic zenith, in a period of intellectual consummation unique in world history.

Athens was the womb of western civilisation. A host of Greek words and ideas, such as democracy, harmony, music, mathematics, art, gastronomy, architecture, logic, eros, euphoria, among others, enriched a multitude of languages, and inspired civilisations.

Over the years, a multitude of conquerors occupied Athens, and erected unique, splendid monuments - a rare historical palimpsest.

In 1834 Athens became the capital of the modern Greek state. The choice was based on the symbolic significance of Athens' classical history. In two centuries since Athens has become an attractive modern metropolis with unrivalled charm.

Athens offers visitors a unique experience. A "journey" in its 6,000-year history, including the chance to see renowned monuments and masterpieces of art of the antiquity and the Middle Ages, and the architectural inheritance of the 19th and 20th centuries. You get an uplifting feeling of snugness in the brilliant light of the attic sky, surveying the charming landscape in the environs of the city (the indented coastline, beaches and mountains), and enjoying the modern infrastructure of the city and unique verve of the Athenians.

Year-round visitors are fascinated by the attractions of Athens.

Eclecticism

In the late 19th century the tradition of neoclassicism was enriched by the romantic aesthetic, usually following the French style. Although Athenian classicism remained the predominant architectural style, public and private buildings were constructed in this period in a breezy style, influenced by the decorative style in vogue in Western Europe.

Art Nouveau

This radical movement was not established as a major architectural trend in Athens. However, after 1920, Greek bourgeois from Smyrna, Egypt, and Constantinople constructed residences following the art nouveau style. The few, impressive art nouveau buildings contrasted with the uniform neoclassical and eclectic architecture prevailing in Athens.

▲

2. University of Athens: a superb example of neo-classical architecture.

Neoclassicism

was from 1834 to the 1920's the predominant architectural style of the small city – which was situated in what is today the historical centre. The style of neoclassicism, which was in vogue in Western Europe, was a product of the romantic fascination with antiquity. It was introduced by German architects who came to Greece in the early 1830's to plan Athens. In the interwar era and especially after 1955, a number of Athens' neoclassical buildings were torn down. However, in many areas of the historical centre, the charming, neoclassical style has been preserved.

▶

3. Distinctive art nouveau mansions at Vassilisis Sofias Avenue.

The modernist movement

In the early 1930's, buildings with more than two or three floors – the usual number of floors of buildings at the time -

4. In the period from 1930-1960 a multitude of buildings reflecting architectural trends from modernism to more recent styles were built in Athens.

were constructed. These small blocks of flats, which sometimes had six floors, introduced a Greek variety of the international modernist architectural style (Bauhaus, Art Deco). The main characteristic of buildings constructed in this period, (as well as the preceding period), are the semicircular ledges, and the facades. A multitude of these buildings are thought to be important monuments exemplifying the global history of the modernist style.

The post-war era (1950 - 2000).

In the post-war era, the population of Athens and demand for housing rapidly increased. In the 1950's and the early 1960's, buildings with marble facades, parapets, and imposing entrances were in vogue. From 1960-1975 (the development era) the mass construction of dull modern buildings was in vogue, altering the physiognomy of the new neighbourhoods. Quality buildings were also constructed in this era. In the past few decades, following a period of stagnation, Athens has acquired important new (predominantly public) buildings, giving the city a new splendour, and upgrading depressed areas.

5. The building of the Headquarters of the National Bank of Greece, one of the most modern buildings in Athens (2002). ▼

5

Tour of Athens, stage 1:

ANTIQUITIES IN ATHENS

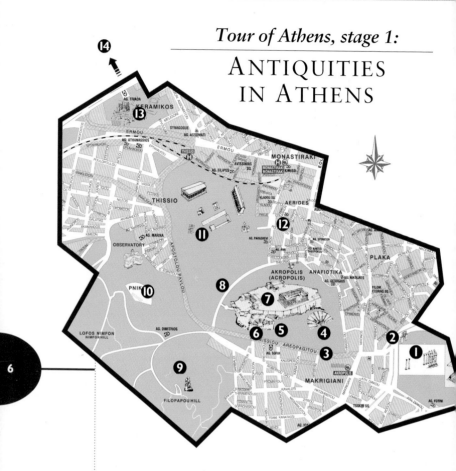

6

A 3-kilometre pedestrian zone (the biggest in Europe) has been established in central roads (Vas. Olgas Str, D. Aeropaghitou Str, Ap. Pavlou Str, Adrianou Str. and a section of Ermou Str.) leading to the major archaeological sites of Athens (archaeological park). Visitors to the section from Dionysiou Aeropaghitou (opposite Hadrian's Arch) to the crossroads of Ermou Str and Piraeus Str (in the Kerameikos area, the location of the third square, according to the first urban design of modern Athens) may enjoy the ancient landscape in a tranquil setting city. **The archaeological tour is a unique experience.**

❶ THE TEMPLE OF OLYMPIAN ZEUS

According to geographer, Pausanias, the temple of Olympian Zeus was founded by Deukalionas, a mythical ancestor of the Greeks. In the age of tyrany, circa 515 BC, Peisistratos the younger grandson of the tyrant Peisistratos, attempted to replace the old temple with a new, more impressive temple. The tyranny, however, was abolished and construction work was terminated. The construction of the new temple was later assigned to the Roman architect Decimus Cossutius by the king of Syria Antiochos IV Epiphanes. Antiochos died in 163 BC and the construction of the temple was once again abandoned. The structure did not have a roof and pediment. The construction of the temple, which ranks among the biggest in antiquity, was completed in 131 AD by the Roman Emperor Hadrian.

▪ **Ilissos Valley.** The surviving section of the Ilissos river valley (near the temple of Olympian Zeus) is worth a visit. In antiquity the Ilissos river was known as the sacred river of the Muses. Scattered remains of ancient sanctuaries are located in the valley. You will find nearby the rock of the Kalliroi spring – which was famous in antiquity – and the church of *Ayia Fotini*, which was built in 1872 at the site of an ancient temple, on the foundation of the sacred sanctuary of Ekati. You will find nearby, the preserved monuments of the classical, Roman, and Byzantine age, among others, *(the Temple of Apollo Delphinios, the Temple of Cronos and Rhea, a Byzantine quarter with work-shops, and Leonidis Church).*

❷ HADRIAN'S ARCH

Following the construction of the temple of Zeus, the Athenians, in 131 AD, in honour of Hadrian, built an arch on the northwestern perimeter of the temple. The arch, built of Pentelic marble, bears two inscriptions on the architrave over the arch. One inscription, facing the Acropolis and the old town (facing west), says: "This is Athens, the city of Theseus." The other inscription, facing the sanctuary and an extension of Athens constructed by Hadrian, (facing east), says: "This is the city of Hadrian, not Theseus.

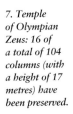

6. Hadrian's arch, the symbolic gate of the city of Athens.

◀

7. Temple of Olympian Zeus: 16 of a total of 104 columns (with a height of 17 metres) have been preserved.

❸ DIONYSIOU AEROPAGHITOU STR.

Dionysiou Aeropaghitou Str. is one of the most impressive streets of Athens, offering a fantastic view of the rock of the Acropolis and the Parthenon. Most of the buildings on one side of the road facing south were constructed in the late 19th century and the early 20th century in the neoclassical or modernist style, reflecting the bourgeois style of the street.

❹ THE ANCIENT THEATRE OF DIONYSOS

Directions: Enter the archaeological area on the southern slope of the Acropolis (entrance at Dionysiou Aeropaghitou Str.), and descend. On the slope to your right is the most ancient theatre of the world, the Theatre of Dionysos. In this theatre, the most famous ancient Greek

poets, Aeschylos, Aristophanes, Euripides, and Sophocles saw premiere performances of their plays in the 5th century BC. The auditorium and the proscenium were made of wood. In the 4th century BC they were reconstructed using marble. Sections of the stone auditorium survive. According to experts, the theatre had a capacity of 17,000. On the slope overlooking the theatre, sculpted on the rock of the Acropolis, is the donated *Monument of Thasyllus* (319 BC) and two donated *Corinthian columns.*

8

8. The Theatre of Dionysos.

9. *Famous sights of Athens: the floodlit rock of the Acropolis, the Parthenon, the Erechtheion, the Temple of Athena Victory and the Propylaea. In the foreground, the Roman Odeion of Herodes Atticus and in the background Lycavittos hill.*

❺ THE STOA OF EUMENES

Above the theatre is the Stoa of Eumenes, which was built by the King of Pergamon, Eumenes II in the 2nd century BC. The arch provided shelter to theatregoers in case of bad weather or shade from the sun. Above the Stoa are the ruins of the *Asklepieion* of Athens, which was built in 429 BC, following the plague, which decimated the population.

❻ THE ODEION OF HERODES ATTICUS

The Odeion of Herodes Atticus was built in 161 AD by the wealthy Herodes Tiverius Claudius Atticus, a teacher and philosopher, who inherited a fortune from his father. Herodes Atticus constructed the covered Odeion in memory of his wife Rigilla. Ancient Greeks organised events in the Odeion. The Odeion is a venue for festivities of the Athens Festival (➡ page 120). You may enjoy the beauty and charm of the Odeion in a morning stroll on the way to the Acropolis.

10. *The performance of a ballet on the stage at the Odeion of Herodes Atticus.*

7.1 ➤ THE PROPYLAEA

adorned with monuments, is the grand entrance of the Acropolis. The Propylaea, built by Pericles in 437-432 BC, were the work of the famous Athenian architect, Mnesikles.

11. The northern wing of the Propylaea, known as the Gallery, was decorated with paintings.

10

❼ THE ACROPOLIS

The Acropolis is the symbol of Athens, the sacred rock, linking the fabulous ancient civilisation with the modern city.
The monuments on the Sacred Rock date back to the prehistoric era and antiquity. The grandeur and beauty of the Sacred Rock attract Greek and foreign visitors. A visit to the Acropolis is a unique experience.

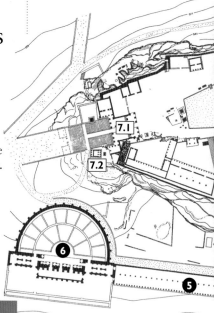

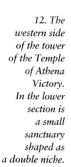

12. The western side of the tower of the Temple of Athena Victory. In the lower section is a small sanctuary shaped as a double niche.

7.2 ➤ THE TEMPLE OF THE ATHENA NIKE (Apteros Nike)

south of the Propylaea, was built was built circa 420 BC in commemoration of the victory of the Greeks against the Persians. The temple was the work of the architect Kallikrates. The site was the location of a sanctuary in the prehistoric era. To the left of the temple you will find the Erechtheion. Facing the temple is the Parthenon.

7.3 ➤ THE PARTHENON

is an architectural masterpiece of great renown. You will appreciate its splendour if you visit, and learn about the

the classical temple, which was constructed and decorated from 447-432BC (in the Golden Age of Pericles), were Iktinos and

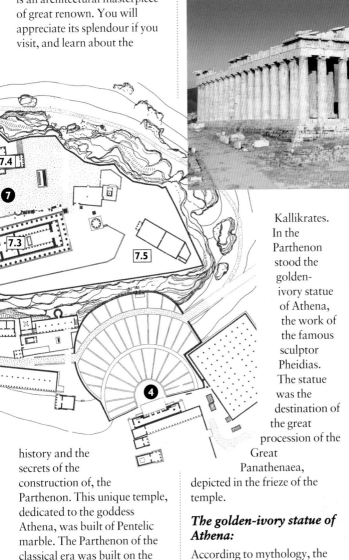

Kallikrates. In the Parthenon stood the golden-ivory statue of Athena, the work of the famous sculptor Pheidias. The statue was the destination of the great procession of the Great Panathenaea, depicted in the frieze of the temple.

history and the secrets of the construction of, the Parthenon. This unique temple, dedicated to the goddess Athena, was built of Pentelic marble. The Parthenon of the classical era was built on the remains of the monumental earlier Parthenon, an archaic temple built in the late 6th century BC. The architects of

The golden-ivory statue of Athena:

According to mythology, the name of the city is connected with a rivalry between Poseidon and Athena for the guardianship of the city.

▲
13. The Parthenon, the most splendid architectural achievement of classical Greece.

11

Poseidon offered the Athenians a horse, while Athena, struck the rock of the Acropolis with her spear, and an olive tree sprouted. The Athenians preferred the olive tree, which symbolised peace and prosperity. The city was named after Athena. The 12-metre high statue stood in the Parthenon. The interior of the statue was made of wood, while the nude parts were made of ivory. The removable robe and the helmet were coated with gold plating. The statue, which represented the goddess Athena bearing arms, and on her right hand a 2-metre high ivory statue of victory, was lost in the early Byzantine era. Ancient sources, and the analytical descriptions of Pausanias (2nd century AD), testify to the existence of the statue. Archaeologists have derived information about the statue from copies. The most famous copy is the Varvakeios Athena.

12

14. The Erechtheion, on the northern side of the rock of the Acropolis.

> ### Take note of the following:
>
> *Please be patient when you ascend the holy rock. You will be rewarded by the spectacular view at the top.*
>
> • You will pass through the Propylaea before you arrive at the Parthenon.
>
> • The view from the temple of the Athena Nike is spectacular.
>
> • The slight bulge of the columns of the Parthenon gives the impression that they are bending under the weight of the roof.
>
> • The secret of the harmony of the Parthenon is that there is not a straight line in the design.

7.4 ➤ THE ERECHTHEION

was built from 420-406 BC at the most holy site of the Acropolis, where goddess Athena planted the olive tree, her sacred symbol. The tree was later destroyed by Persian invaders. According to mythology, following the expulsion of the Persians, the tree miraculously sprouted again.

Caryatids: The figures of the maidens supporting the roof of the southern balcony of the temple are copies. Five of the

Don't be deceived by the optical illusion of the columns, which appear to bulge.

- The Erechtheion is a unique temple constructed according to the style of ancient Athens. It is constructed on two levels. It is asymmetrical and has two balconies, which are not thematically connected to each other. The small balcony on the south side is better known, mainly due to the six Caryatids that support the roof. The differences between the sections of the temple may be due to the fact that the various parts are dedicated to various gods. The eastern section was dedicated to Athena Poliada, and the western section to Poseidon Erechtheus.

six Maidens that once adorned the temple are displayed in the Acropolis Museum, while the sixth is displayed in the British Museum.

7.5 ➤ THE ACROPOLIS MUSEUM

displays the priceless finds of the Acropolis, the most important religious centre of the city of Athens, and presents its history and function. The most important exhibits are:

The Moschoforos:
The exceptional statue of a bearded youth (6th century BC) carrying a calf on his shoulders for sacrifice to Athena.

The Archaic Kores:
The statues of maidens sacrificed to Athena. No two Kores were alike. The varying styles of their hair and the drapery of their robes are prime examples of the development of sculpture in ancient Greece.

Sculptures decorating the Parthenon (444-432BC):
The sculptures are the remnants of an all-time masterpiece. Among others, you will find sections of the frieze depicting the Olympian gods, and certain metopes depicting a scene of the Battle of the Centaurs (Centauromachia).

The Caryatids:
The statues of the beautiful priestesses supported the roof of the southern balcony of the Erechtheion (420 BC). Apparently they were named after the women of Caryes (an ancient city of Arcadia in the Peloponnese), who are thought to have been the models of certain statues. In the Ottoman era the Caryatids were also called Petrified Princesses or the Girls of the Castle.

13

▲
15. Varvakeios Athena, a copy of Pheidias's golden-ivory statue (National Archaeological Museum).

16. The southern balcony of the Erechtheion with the famous Caryatids.

17. The Acropolis Museum: The "child of Kritias" (circa 480 B.C.), found in the mid-19th century in the vicinity of the Parthenon.

▶

❽ THE AREIOS PAGOS

The Areios Pagos, venerated in antiquity, is the most ancient law court of the world. It was the seat of the first aristocratic assembly of ancient Athens. The assembly gradually lost political influence and in the latter half of the 5th century, it retained solely its function as a court, mostly hearing murder cases. The Oresteia describes the trial at this court of Orestes for the murder of his mother Clytemnaestra, and her lover Aegisthus. Apostle Paul spoke to the Athenians at the Areios Pagos in 51 AD. A bronze plaque on the base of the rock commemorates his sermons.

❾ PHILOPAPPOU HILL

Well worth a visit any time of the year. A walk at Philopappou Hill is a fascinating experience: you will find here a unique copse, monuments thought to have been the *"Prisons of Socrates,"* the *"Tombs of Kimon,"* and the *"Iroo Mousaiou,"* the Philopappou Monument and the spectacular view of the Parthenon and the magnificent monuments of the Acropolis.

☞ THE SIGHTS:

- **Philopappou Monument** was built by Athenians in the 2nd century BC in honour of the benefactor, ruler of Syria, Gaius Julius Antiochus. Gaius Julius was also known as Philopappos, which roughly translated means "beloved grandchild." His grandfather was the last King of Kommagene Antiochus IV.

- **Cobbled road.** In the 1950's the Greek architect D. Pikionis developed the design of the area encompassing the Prolylaea of the Acropolis and Philopappou Hill. Take note of

18. Philopappou Hill: the cobbled footpaths of D. Pikionis.

14

the hand made cobbled roads leading to the monuments, the church of Ayios Demetrios Loumbardiaris (●◆ *page 23*) and the refreshment room.

The area has been designated a Scheduled and Protected Monument of the Global Cultural Heritage.

⑩ THE PNYX

The Pnyx is situated between *the Hill of the Muses* (the location of Philopappou Monument) and *the Hill of the Nymphs*, (the location of the Sanctuary of the Nymphs and the National Observatory, ●◆ *page 43*). The semicircular square was after 6th century BC the location of the assembly of the people of Athens. They gathered here to hear orators speak from a rock platform in the centre of the Pnyx, and participate in the democratic polity. The assembly is thought to have a capacity of 10,000.

⑪ THE ANCIENT AGORA

The archaeological area of the ancient Agora is located on the foothills of the Acropolis, near metro stop "Theseion." In antiquity, the Agora was not solely a commercial centre. It was also an important political, cultural and religious centre. In the area of the agora were located administrative buildings, temples, public services and courts. The Athenians gathered here every day to buy and sell their goods, learn the current news, criticise the government, exchange ideas, or engage in discussion. The area was settled in the Neolithic age. The monuments located there that were built in various historical periods: from the classical age to the 11th century AD. The church of Ayioi Apostoloi was built in the 11th century AD (●◆ *page 22*).

19. The funerary monument of Philopappou (with a height of 12 metres), decorated with sculpted depictions of Philopappou and his family.

◄

15

20. Pnyx: the speaker's podium, facing the rock of the Acropolis.

LY

II.3

21. The Temple of Hephaistos ("Theseion"), on the northern side of the Ancient Agora (Agoraeios Kolonos hill).

16

22. A model of the monument of the Eponymous Heroes.

☞ THE SIGHTS:

II.1 ➤ **Theseion – Temple of Hephaistos.** The Theseion was dedicated to Hephaistos and Athena, and not Theseus. It is located in the western perimeter of the Agora. It is the best-preserved temple of antiquity. It was built in 460-415 BC. In the temple were statues of Hephaistos and Athena, thought to have been sculpted by Alkamenes.

II.2 ➤ **The monument of the Eponymous Heroes.** Here stood the statues of the ten heroes of Attica (4th century BC). The ten tribes of Attica were named after the heroes. Public announcements were displayed on the pedestal of these statues.

II.3 ➤ **Poikile Stoa.** It is thought that the Poikile Stoa derived its name from the variety of the colours and themes of its frescoes. The name "Poikile" (in greek poikile means diverse) leads us to the supposition that the frescoes here were painted in a variety of colours and themes. Here Zenon taught Stoic philosophy, which was named after the Poikile Stoa (460 BC).

II.4 ➤ **The Stoa of Attalos.** The Stoa of Attalos, a two-floor building, was donated by the King of Pergamon Attalos II (159-138 BC) to the city of Athens. It is thought to have been a kind of ancient commercial centre with 21 shops on each floor. The collection of the Museum displays everyday objects, which were unearthed in excavations in the ancient Agora. Visitors may get an idea of everyday life ancient Athens.

II.5 ➤ **The Basileios Stoa.** The Basileios Stoa, constructed crica 500 BC, is located on the foothills of the Theseion. It was the seat of the Archon Vasileus and the council of the Areios Pagos.

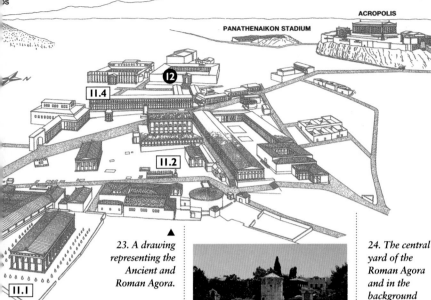

23. A drawing representing the Ancient and Roman Agora.

24. The central yard of the Roman Agora and in the background Kyristes' Clock ("The tower of the winds").

17

⑫ THE ROMAN AGORA

The Roman Agora (in the Plaka area) was an architectural complex consisting of a large rectangular court surrounded by colonnades (stoa). Behind the stoas were various shops. North of the complex was a *library* (a rectangular building; the dimensions of the building are 122x82 m), which was built by Hadrian in 132 AD.

☞ THE SIGHTS:

■ **Kyristes' Clock - Tower of the Winds.** On the eastern side of the Roman Agora stands an octagonal monument. The Clock of Andronicus Kyrristus, constructed in the 1st century BC, was a hydraulic clock. On each face of the clock can be seen bas-reliefs of the eight winds. The name has taken its name 'Winds' from the depictions.

◄

25. Attalos Colonnade was fully restored from 1953-1956. It houses the Ancient Agora Museum.

⓭ THE KERAMEIKOS

The ancient Kerameikos was located in the northwestern outskirts of ancient Athens. It was part enclosed by, and part beyond, the walls that divide the area of the excavation. In the centre of the archaeological area are the two best known arches of ancient Athens, the **Dipylon** and the **Sacred Arch**. In the vicinity of the arches was the most ancient and the biggest cemetery of Attica. Moreover it was the place of burial of citizens who were honoured by the city of Athens. According to the geographer Pausanias, the location was named after Keramos.

26. The stele of Hegeso.

However, the place was most likely named after the neighbourhood of the kerameoi (potters). (The definition of Kerameikos is something related to ceramics of potters). The neighbourhood of the kerameoi was established on the banks of the **river Iridanos**. You can see the riverbed in the archaeological area. The ancient Demos of Kerameikos covered a large area. Only part of it has been unearthed in excavations. It is thought that the area of the Kerameikos was bounded by the northwestern perimeter of the Agora on one side and the copse that was named after the hero Akademos.

18

27. Dexileos's funerary monument. Dexileos was killed in 394 B.C. in a battle near Corinth.

The festival of the Panathenaea.

Every year the ancient Athenians celebrated the Mikra (lesser) Panathenaea, and every four years they celebrated the Megala (great) Panathenaea, which were grander and included horse racing, athletic contests, competitions in music and other arts. On the last day of the festival, a procession began at Kerameikos, passed the Agora and ascended the Acropolis, where a robe named after Athena was offered to the goddess. According to custom, during the festival statues were

☞ THE SIGHTS:

■ **Tombs and stelae (columns).** The Kerameikos is mainly known for its tombs and columns. The copy of the marble bull in the enclosure of the tomb of Dionysos from Kollytos, and the copy of the famous stele of Dexileos and Hegeso (late 5th century BC). If you want to see the original sculptures, and other finds of the excavation, you may visit the Museum, at the archaeological site.

■ **The Kerameikos Museum.** The museum displays the finds of the excavation of Kerameikos, including funeral gifts found in tombs and scruptures adorning tombs of the archaic and classical periods.

■ **The Public Memorial.** A section of the ancient cemetery, including the tombs of public figures and a multitude of the graves of soldiers fallen in battle, was recently excavated near the archaeological area of Kerameikos (at Salaminas Str 35).

covered with real clothes. The robe of the gods was basically a woollen tunic, selected by a priestess and young virgins assisting her. It was placed on the mast of a large wooden boat as its sail and carried to the Acropolis. The procession followed the boat. The procession is depicted on the frieze of Acropolis.

⑭ THE AKADEMIA PLATONOS (PLATO ACADEMY)

The area was settled in the prehistoric age (in the 6th century BC one of the three famous Gymnasia of Athens was founded here). It is named after the hero Akademos, or Ekademos. However, it is known after the famous philosophical school founded by Plato *(neighbourhood Akademia Platonos)* in 387 BC. The school was a focal point of the prestigious Neoplatonist philosophers.

☞ THE SIGHTS:

■ **The Sacred Residence of the geometric years** consists of seven rectangular spaces. It has the same features as the sacred residence of Eleusina. Remnants of sacrifices found at the residence seem to indicate that intensive worship took place here.

■ **The Gymnasium.** The Gymnasium is a large rectangular building (1st century BC – 1 century AD), with an internal peristyle and rooms on the northern side. In the Gymnasium is a small area that served as an arena.

■ **The Peristyle building.** A large rectangular building (4th century BC) with an interior peristyle. It is thought to be an arena or an annex of the Gymnasium.

■ **The Early Greek Arched Residence.** It consists of a hall, a chamber and a storage room. It is thought to be the prehistoric residence of Akademos.

Tour of Athens, stage 2:

BYZANTINE MONUMENTS IN ATHENS

The 11th and the 12th centuries are thought to be **the Golden Age of Athens' Byzantine art.** Most of the better known and more important Byzantine churches of Athens were built in these two centuries as part of a Christian reconstruction following the campaigns of Emperor Basil II in the Balkans. Some of the better-known monasteries were also founded in the same period in the suburbs of Athens.

20

☞ **THE SIGHTS:**

❶ THE OLD METROPOLIS (THE OLD CATHEDRAL)
(Metropoleos Square)

This charming church is located near the new Cathedral. It was built in the late 12th century. It is dedicated to Gorgoepikoos Panavia (the Virgin Mary) and Ayios Eleftherios. Ancient and Byzantine bas-reliefs were used for the construction of the church. In the façade is an ancient frieze, taken from a monument of the 4th century depicting official attic festivals. The church was the official

Episcopal Sea of Athens following the expulsion of the bishops from the Parthenon by the Franks and later the Turks. From 1839 to 1842 it was used as a library. The new Metropolis nearby was built from 1842 and 1862 as the cathedral of Athens. It is a domed church built in the neobyzantine and neoclassical style.

28. Kapnikarea.

was a hindrance to traffic. However, thanks to the intervention of Ludwig of Bavaria, father of King Otto, and Neofytos Metaxas, Bishop of Talantio and Vicar of Athens, the church was preserved at the present location.

❸ AYIOS NIKOLAOS RANGAVAS *(Plaka)*

is located near the Anafiotika area of Plaka. The church was built in the 11th century. It was part of the Palace of the Rangavas family. Michael I, Emperor of Byzantium, was descended from this family. The area around the church was formerly called Rangavas.

29. Ayios Eleftherios.

❷ KAPNIKAREA
(Ermou Str.)

The Kapnikarea is a cruciform, domed church with a dome dedicated to the Presentation of the Virgin Mary. The original building was constructed in the 11th century. Construction was completed in the 13 century BC. It has had various names: Camoucharea, Chryssocamouchariotissa, Panayia tis Vasilopoulas (Virgin of the King's daughter). In 1834, the year of the construction of Ermou Str, the authorities considered plans to relocate the church, or demolish it, since it was located in the middle of Ermou Str, and

21

❼ METOCHI PANA-YIOU TAFOU
(Anafiotika)

It is located at Erechtheos Str. It is a small monastery belonging to the Holy Sepulchre of Jerusalem. The church of the monastery, Ayioi Anarghyroi was built in the 17th century.

❽ PANAYIA CHRYS-SOKASTRIOTISSA
(Anafiotika)

One of several churches in Anafiotika. According to popular belief, the miraculous icon of the church protects believers in difficult circumstances.

❾ SOTIRA LYKODIMOU - Russian Church
(Filellinon Str.)

is the biggest medieval building of Athens. Built in 1031, it was part of a Roman Catholic monastery that closed in 1701. In the 1850's the building was renovated by Tsar Alexander II who donated a bell-tower. Sotiras Lykodimos is the Russian Orthodox Church of Athens.

❿ AYIOI APOSTOLOI TOU SOLAKI
(Ancient Agora)

is located in the compound of the Ancient Agora excavation. It is one of the oldest churches of Athens (1000-1025 BC). It was constructed on the ruins of a Roman nympheum of the 2nd century. In the 1950's, following a renovation, it was

❹ AYIA EKATERINI
(Plaka)

is located near the Lyssikrates Monument, in Lyssikratous Square. Shading the church is a palm tree. It was constructed from 11th-12th century. In the corner of the square are the ruins of a roman monument.

❺ AYIOS IOANNIS THEOLOGOS
(Plaka)

is a very beautiful cruciform church of the 11th-12th century. It is located at the crossroads of Erotokritou Str. and Erechtheos Str. It has been renovated several times.

❻ SOTIRA TOU KOTAKI
(Plaka)

is better known as Ayia Sotira. It is located at Kydathenaeon Str, opposite the Museum of Greek Folk art, in the Plaka area. It was built in the 11th-12th century. It has been renovated several times.

22

▲
30. The Byzantine church of Ayioi Apostoloi, on the eastern side of the Ancient Agora.

restored to its original form. Many post-Byzantine frescoes of church of Ayios Spyridonas, which has been demolished, were transported to Ayioi Apostoloi.

⑪ PANTANASSA
(Monastiraki Square)

Built in the 10th century, the church belonged to the monastery of the Koimesi tis Theotokou. The neighbour-hood was named after the monastery. Formerly it was a monastery dependency of the Kaisariani Monastery.

⑫ AYIOS DEMETRIOS LOUMBARDIARIS
(Philopappou Hill)

is a beautiful church of the 16th century, with remarkable frescoes. According to popular belief, the name (Loumbardiaris of Bombardiaris) was derived

from an incident that occurred in the 17th century. Ayios Demetrios protected believers from a great cannon (Loumbarda).

⑬ AYIOI ASOMATOI
(Theseion)

A cruciform church built in the 11th century.

⑭ AYIOS IOANNIS STIN KOLONA
(Euripidou Str.)

A small chapel built in the 12th century, it was named after a Roman column, preserved in the interior. Ayios Ioannis o Vaptistis was thought to be a healer of all sicknesses of the head. Visitors may see on the column offerings to the Saint offered by the faithful expressing gratitude for his help.

23

31. *Ayios Demetrios Loumbardiaris, on Philopappus hill.*

⓰ AYIOI THEODOROI
(Klathmonos Square)

The church was reconstructed in the late 11th century on the foundation of a church that was built in the 9th century. It was built by N. Kalomaos, who was a Spatharocandidatos (a rank of the Byzantine Court).

32. Byzantine mosaic of the Virgin. Constantinople, 10th century (Benaki Museum).

⓰ TAXIARCHES
(the church of the Petraki Monastery, at 14, Gennadiou Str.)

built in the 12th century, it belongs to the Petraki Monastery (18th century). In the cross-domed church visitors may see frescoes dating back to 1719.

⓱ AYIOI ISIDOROI
(Lycavittos hill)

is a small church located in a large cave in Lycavittos Hill. It was formerly called Ayios Sidereas church. It was burned in 1930 and reconstructed in 1931.

⓲ AYIOS GEORGIOS
(Lycavittos hill)

is a whitewashed church at the top of Lycavittos hill. You can reach the church on foot, or by funicular. It is thought that in antiquity the temple of Akraios Zeus was located here. In the period of Frankish rule, the small chapel of Profitis Ilias was built here. Later Ayios Georgios the Rider was built here. The exact date of the construction of the church is not known. The church bell was donated by Queen Olga who put the ruined church under her protection.

24

33. Ayios Georgios, on the top of Lycavittos hill. In the background is its distinctive bell tower.

Tour of Athens, stage 3:

OTTOMAN MONUMENTS IN ATHENS

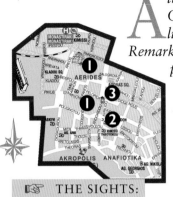

Athens was conquered by the Ottomans in 1456 and liberated in 1833. Remarkable buildings of the period have been preserved.

34. The Tzistarakis Mosque, on the picturesque Monastiraki Square.

☞ THE SIGHTS:

❶ MOSQUES

The **Tzistaraki Mosque** (or Kato Sintrivaniou), located in Monastiraki Square, was built in 1759 by the Turkish voivod Moustafa Agas (or Tzistarakis). Seeking lime for the construction of the Mosque, Tzistarakis removed the 17th column of the Temple of Olympian Zeus (👉 page 7). The Mosque has a loggia with four columns and two rows of four windows on each side. Since 1981 it has housed the Museum of Traditional Ceramics. In Athens, there is only one mosque open to the public, the Tzistaraki Mosque. Near the Roman Agora (👉 page 17), is the remarkable **Fetihie Mosque**, built in 1458 in honour of Mohamed II the Conqueror, on the occasion of his visit to Athens.

❷ TURKISH BATH

The Old Bath *(Hamam Abit Efendi)*, in Plaka (at 8, Kyrristou Str.), built in the 17th century, was a popular meeting place in the Ottoman era. The Old Bath has been renovated. It houses the *Personal Hygiene and Toilet Museum.*

❸ MUSLIM SEMINARY

The gate of the Muslim seminary, at the crossroads of Aeolou Str. and Pelopida Str, is the remains of the building, which was destroyed in a fire in 1911. According to an inscription above the entrance, the seminary was built in 1721 and consisted of a main building, which was a school and mosque, buildings housing the students and teachers (hodjia), kitchen and hygiene areas, and a central court.

25

35. The gate of the Muslim seminary (mendreses).

Tour of Athens,
stage 4:

HISTORIC CENTRE (1)

36. *Traditional taverna in the Plaka. There are a multitude of tavernas in the district.*

❶ PLAKA

Plaka, also known as the "neighbourhood of the gods," is one of the oldest neighbourhoods of Athens. Walking on its paved narrow streets you get the feeling that you are travelling back in time. The origin of the name of the neighbourhood is unknown, although theories abound. According to popular belief, Plaka was named after a slab of stone that was found near the church of Ayios Georgios Alexandrias, in the vicinity of the theatre of Dionysos. The beautiful neoclassical style colour of the houses, the architecture, the well-kept gardens, and the beauty and atmosphere of the neighbourhood are enchanting. In Plaka the air you breathe is different; it is lighter, cleaner, and fragrant, like a gift of the gods. When you visit Plaka you should bring a map, because you might get lost in the labyrinth of narrow streets and alleys.

1.1 ➤ PHILOMOUSOU ETAIREIAS SQUARE

The central square of the neighbourhood, was named after the Philomousos Etaireia (The Society of the Friends of the Muses, in other words, the nine gods of the Arts), which was founded in 1813. The purpose of the Society was the promotion of Greek studies and the preservation of the archaeological treasures of Athens. At the square, located at the crossroads of Kydathenaeon Str, Farmaki Str, Olympiou Dios Str. and Angelou Geronda Str, are a multitude of cafes, restaurants, clubs with live music and souvenir shops.

1.2 ➤ THE CHILDRENS MUSEUM

located at Kidathenaeon Str. is a wonderful place for children. In the attic is a reconstructed room with old furniture, a radio, and theatre in the style of old Athenian homes, named "granddad and grandmother's room," where children may dress with period dresses. The Museum houses among others, an exhibition of paintings by children, old toys, a fairground and a library. If you have children, be sure to visit the Children's Museum.

1.3 ➤ Towards the Acropolis
LYSIKRATES MONUMENT

In ancient Athens, theatrical performances held at the theatre of Dionysos were funded by wealthy citizens, the donors (choregoi). The city gave a prize to the donor of the winning performance. When the wealthy Lysikrates won the prize in 334 BC, he constructed a monument to house it. The monument is preserved (*ancient Tripodon Str.* - pavement of the road is preserved in a special

37. Handmade wooden toy representing a bridegroom on horseback. The design is derived from an embroidery of the 18th century. (Benaki Museum).

27

38. Lysikrates Monument.

space in a renovated building at number 28). The monument has had a long and varied history. In 1658, a Capuchin monastery was founded here. In 1669, Capuchins bought the monument. Lord Byron stayed at the monastery in his second visit to Greece. In the gardens the cultivation of the tomato, hitherto unknown in Greece, was introduced.

39. Wooden window decorated with flowerpots in the "neighbourhood of the gods."

1.4 > **ANAFIOTIKA**

On the foothills of the Acropolis, has the charm of a beautiful island village. It was built by the renowned builders of the Aegean island of Anafi, who were invited to construct the palace of the first king of the Hellenes, Otto. Feeling nostalgic for their birthplace in their long stay in Athens they recreated it in the upper area of Plaka. They built small, whitewashed houses, reproducing the architectural style of their village. We recommend that you visit Anafiotika, the neighbourhood of the Anafiotes, a unique, charming area.

▪ **The Museum of the University of Athens**

The building housing the Museum of Athens, located at Tholou Str, was formerly the residence of the architect Kleanthes (1832-1833). Subsequently it housed the first University of Athens (1837-1842).

28

40. A multitude of the labyrinthine alleys of the Plaka lead to the Anafiotika and the peripheral footpath of the Acropolis.

■ The Kanellopoulos Museum

Was founded in 1976, following the donation of the private collection of Pavlos and Alexandra Kanellopoulos to the Greek state. It is housed in the neoclassical mansion of the Mihalea family. The Kanello-poulos collection consists of archaeological finds and works of art from the prehistoric era to the present.

❷ MONASTIRAKI

A distinctive "old" Athens street, with narrow, irregularly criss-crossing streets, and small buildings, characteristic of Ottoman and to some extent Byzantine urban planning. On the outdoor stands of street sellers, or the small shops on the central roads *(Adrianou Str, Pandrosou Str, Ifaistou Str, Thiseiou Str, Ayiou Filippou Str, Astigos Str, and Ermou Str.)* you can find anything, such as shoes, clothes, old and new furniture, old books and magazines, souvenirs, jewellery, hats, bronze objects, new and used records and CDs and traditional Greek instruments (bouzoukis, touberleki). Shopping or walking in Monastiraki is an unforgettable experience. You will be stunned by the variety and quality of things you can buy in the market.

☞   THE SIGHTS:

2.1 ➤ **MONASTIRAKI SQUARE**

At the historic square you will find the Tzistaraki mosque *(●❖ page 25),* Hadrian's

41. The facades of neo-classical houses in Monastiraki.

library *(●❖ page 17),* the Byzantine church of Pantanassa *(●❖ page 23),* and a completely renovated neoclassical metro station - one of the oldest of the metro network.

30

2.3 ➤ ADRIANOU STR.

A distinctive Athens street, connects Hadrian's library with the "Theseio" metro stop. In the neoclassical one-floor or two-floor buildings are shops with traditional items, and antique shops. Street-sellers sell their ware here Sundays. You will find here cafes and small fashionable restaurants with a unique view of the archaeological area of the Ancient Agora (●◆ page 15).

❸ THE OLD COMMERCE CENTRE

The area encompassed by Metropoleos Str, Athinas Str. and Stadiou Str. is the historic centre of Athens, and the old commercial area. In the area are more than 2,500 shops selling a wide range of products. Pedestrian zones have been established. The historic commercial centre is a quiet area, with a multitude of cafes, small bars and modern restaurants.

2.2 ➤ AVYSINIAS SQUARE (Giousouroum)

Is the central square of Monastiraki. Here you will find a wide range of rare furniture, antiques and the copies of antiques, and a variety of used items. Moreover, you will find old wardrobes, bookcases, frames, mirrors, antique office tables, tables, gramophone records and musical instruments. Come early if you want to shop. Noon is the best time to come if you want to take a look around. You can have a glass of Greek wine or ouzo with Greek snacks - called mezedes - in one of the small shops of the square, and observe the bustle of the bazaar.

▲
42. Tourists enjoying a cafe or a meal at Adrianou Street with a view of the Ancient Agora and the Acropolis.

☞ THE SIGHTS:

3.1 ➤ METROPOLEOS STR.

Connects Syntagma Square with Monastiraki Square. The buildings on the street are built in the neoclassical style. The Old Metropolis (The Old Cathedral) (●◆ page 20) dominates Mitropoleos Square.

On the square are a several cafes. In the colourful Dimopratiriou Square nearby you will find tavernas with traditional Greek food.

3.2 ➤ ERMOU STR.

The street is named after the god Hermes – the protector of trade. Ermou Str. was one of the first streets paved by Kleanthes and Schaubert. More than 60 years, from the late 19th century to the 1960's, it was a centre of women's fashion. It is one of the best areas for shopping in the capital. You will find a variety of silver, among others, candle holders, bowls, vases and jewellery, often hand-made goods produced in Greece, in shops at *Lekka Str*, which connects *Perikleous Str.* and *Kolokotroni Str*, and the nearby arcades. In the section of Ermou Str. closest to Syntagma Square, (up to

Athinas Str.) you will find the Kapnikareas church (➤ page 21). In the section of Ermou Str. closest to Pireaus Str. (from Thiseio to Pireaus Str.) you will find the archaeological area of Kerameikos (➤ page 18).

43. Ermou Street and in the background Parliament.

3.3 ➤ ATHINAS STR.

A central commercial road connecting Omonia Square (➤ page 63) with Monastiraki Square (➤ page 29), it was one of the first main roads constructed in modern Athens. Athinas Str. is busy most times of the day. Most of the shops sell groceries. The fragrance of foods, fruits, herbs and nuts pervades the air. The street has the charm of the bazaars of the East. It faces the Acropolis. A multitude of important buildings of the 19th century and the early 20th century is located

44. The Metropolis (Athens Cathedral) at Metropoleos Square. On the right is Ayios Eleftherios chapel.

31

45. The Athens Town Hall.

here. Recently the street has become a centre for Fine Arts with more than ten art galleries in the area.

3.4 ➤ Athens Town Hall
(63, Athinas Str.)

was constructed in 1874 in a strictly neoclassical style. Originally a two-floor building, in 1937 a floor was added and the building was modified due to the increased space requirements of the Municipality. In the interior you will find the paintings of known Greek painters of the 19th century, and frescoes of F. Kontoglou with representations of mythological and historic themes (1937-1940). You will find a large oil painting depicting the Apostle Paul teaching the Athenians Christian religion (1877) in the Municipal Council hall. In the reception room (1st floor), you will find in special glass-showcases, small terra cotta figures representing all the mayors of Athens. In the vicinity of the municipality is an attractive, small square, *Theatrou Square.*

3.5 ➤ Kotzia Square
(National Resistance Square)

Formerly called Laou Square, and Loudovikou Square, faces the Town Hall. The eclectic style *Melas Mansion* (Ern. Ziller 1887), with an impressive façade, and two small towers at the sides, dominates the south side of the square. The central hall is covered with a glass roof. In the perimeter are Doric and Ionian style colonnades. The building, formerly the residence of V. Melas, houses the Cultural Centre of the National Bank of Greece. In the eastern side of the square is a renaissance style building, the *G. Stavrou Mansion,* housing services of the National Bank of Greece. A section of the *Acharnic Gate of the Themistocleian walls* was uncovered and is exhibited in the northeastern section of the square.

3.6 ➤ Varvakeios Municipal (Central) Market

Is a rectangular building (1886) with a large covered court. There are a total of 73 food stalls (meat market, fish market, vegetable market and groceries) in the interior and exterior sections. The market is covered with a glass and metal roof and has symmetrical windows. You will find here small restaurants (eating-houses) with fresh food, attracting Athenians especially after midnight. There is a small grove on the square (Varvakeios Square) across the street.

3.7 ➤ EVRIPIDOU STR.

a charming street with an oriental atmosphere, connects Koumoundourou Square (➤ page 65) with Klafthmonos Square (➤ page 34). You will find here a multitude of shops selling spices, sweets, nuts, coffee, and traditional oriental products.

3.8 ➤ AEOLOU STR.

A pedestrian zone has been established in a large section of the Aiolou Str, which connects Panepistimiou Str. with the Roman Market (Plaka). At the crossroads of Aiolou Str. and Sophocleous Str. is the newly constructed Administration Building of the National Bank of Greece (2002), one of the most important modern architectural sights of Athens. The building was designed by Greek architects, with the collaboration of the famous architect M. Botta. On the ground floor you will find a restored section of the ancient Acharnai road. At 10 Sophocleous Str. is the mansion of the Athens Stock Exchange, with a classical style façade and ten Doric style columns. As you head towards Plaka you will see two marvellous churches, which are well worth a visit: The *Panagia Chrysospiliotissa* (1863 – at the crossroads of Aeolou Str. and Panagia Chrysospiliotissa Str) and Ayias Eirinis Str. (1847- Athinaidos Str.) both built by the architect L. Kaftantzoglou. *Ayia Eirini*, which was the first Cathedral of Athens, is located at a colourful square, with flower shops and cafes.

46. A detail of the central entrance of the G. Stavrou mansion (Kotzia Square).

33

47. The new building of the National Bank of Greece (Aeolou Street).

3.9 ➤ STADIOU STR.

Is a central street – one of the first paved roads of modern Athens. It was built on a river bed. It was formerly called Pheidiou Str. and Akakiou Str. There was a plan to extend the street to the Panathenaean Stadium – which was never put into action – hence the name Stadiou.

48. The Athens Stock Exchange mansion (1930).

3.10 ➤ National Printers Building

Connects Santaroza Str, and Arsaki Str. One of the first public mansions raised in the modern city (1834), it is built in the neoclassical style. Before 1905, it housed the "National Printers."

49. The building housing the cinema halls "Attikon" and Apollon" (1916-1920).

3.11 ➤ Klafthmonos Square

Is a spacious square with interesting buildings (among others, The Museum of the City of Athens ➤ *page 87*, the former Ministry of Merchant Marine, the Ministry of Internal Affairs, the Byzantine church of Ayioi Theodoroi, ➤ *page 24*) and a multitude of cafes. An impressionist bronze statue representing the "National Reconciliation" (Doropoulos 1988) stands in the centre of the square.

3.12 ➤ "Attikon-Apollon" building

Is an eclectic style mansion. It houses two cinemas, among the oldest of Athens, which have recently been renovated.

3.13 ➤ Karytsi Square

Square is a small square, named after the church at its centre. The elegant church (built by L. Kaftantzoglou) was built at the site of an older church where the Athenians in January 1833 selected a deputation to welcome the new king Otto in Nauplion. Opposite the square is the neoclassical style *"Parnassos"* building.

3.14 ➤ Hellenic Telecommunications Organisation (OTE) Mansion

an exceptional example of Athenians modernism, with elements of older architectural styles, it is the work of the known Greek architect An. Metaxas (1931).

3.15 ➤ Kolokotroni Square

a small square, with the Historical and Ethnological Museum and the impressive statue of the hero of the Greek Revolution Th. Kolokotronis on horseback (L. Sohos, 1904) at its centre. Opposite the square (8, Stadiou Str.) is the dilapidated *Douila Residence*, on the oldest buildings of the modern city, the work of Chr. Hansen.

3.16 ➤ The Historical and Ethnological Museum
(➤ page 84).

50. The statue of Th. Kolokotronis before the building of the Historical and Ethnological Museum.

Tour of Athens, stage 5:

HISTORIC CENTRE (2)

51. Distinctive decorative motif on an old building of the historical centre of Athens.

❶ PSYRRI

Acolourful Athens neighbourhood, encompassed by Athinas Str, Ermou Str, and Evripidou Str. It is a busy neighbourhood, especially in the night. You will find on its narrow alleys a multitude of cafes, small bars, clubs, restaurants, ouzo-restaurants, and taverns with live Greek music, theatres, galleries, art galleries, and antique shops.

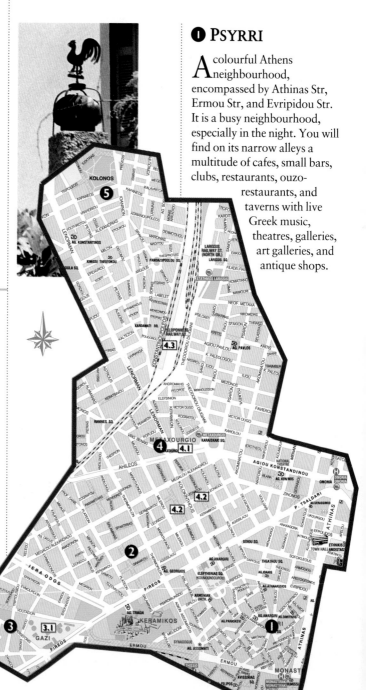

Following the liberation of Greece (1833), veteran freedom fighters and immigrants from the provinces settled in the neighbourhood. They opened cottage industries and workshops, which have given the neighbourhood a distinctive character. In the early 1990s, following a series of construction works, the neighbourhood became a popular nightlife and residential area. *Iroon square*, the central square, is good place for you to start your walk.

52. Two-storey neo-classical building at Iroon Square (Psyri).

❷ KERAMEIKOS

Near the archaeological area (↠ *page 18)* is the historic neighbourhood of Kerameikos. Worth seeing are Ayion Assomaton Str, Melidoni Str. (you will find here the *Jewish synagogue Beth-Shalom* and the *"Museum of Modern Ceramics"*) and Salaminas Str.

53. The Kerameikos neighbourhood around the archaeological site.

☞ THE SIGHTS:

❸ GAZI

The former Gas works is at the centre of the neighbourhood, which was formerly called "Gazohori" (Gas village). Located in western Athens, it is the third square of the city, in accordance with the Kleanthes-Schaubert urban plan. It has to a large extent maintained the colour of a historic Athens neighbourhood. You will find cafes, bars and luxury restaurants, popular among Athenians, in a multitude of old, picturesque buildings.

3.1 ➤ **THE GAS WORKS**

was founded in 1857 and closed in 1983. It produced lighting gas for the city. Formerly in the area were, among others, wood workshops, foundries, machine-works, garages, restaurants, barbers shops, medical centre. The Gas works, a scheduled building, is the only one of its kind in Europe. The buildings have unadorned, neoclassical masonry, a varnished, wooden roof with skylights, covered with Byzantine or French style tiles and sheet-iron. It is an industrial zone, housing a cultural centre of the Athens Municipality ("Technopolis.")

❹ METAXOURGEIO

The historic neighbourhood in the centre of Athens was planned by architect, Chr. Hansen. The name is derived from a silk fabric manufacture factory, which closed in 1875 (the building, which is preserved, is located at Meg. Alexandrou Str, between Mylerou Str. and Giatrakou Str.). On the one side of Achilleos Str. (facing Piraeus

Str.) is the old section, and on the other side (facing Lenorman Str.), is the new section. The new section, which has been reconstructed, has not maintained the historic character of the neighbourhood, while in the old section a number of buildings constructed in the traditional style have been preserved. In the area are a multitude of small cafes and restaurants serving traditional oriental drinks, sweets, and food.

▲
54. A view of the industrial park at Gazi ("Technopolis"), the venue of cultural and other events.

☞ THE SIGHTS:

4.1 ➤ Marble fountain

The marble fountain, located at Metaxourgeio Square, was built in the 19th century. It was transported here from Dimopratiriou Square.

4.2 ➤ Iasonos Str. and Yiatrakou Str.

Starting at Karaiskaki Square, take Achileos Str, turn at Iasonos Str, and proceed to Agisilaou Str. You will find here small theatres in historic buildings. Take a right turn at Akadimou-Yiatrakou Str, and proceed to Achilleos Str. Take note of the small, neoclassical (one-storey and two-story) houses with balconies, balusters, and ornate front doors. At the crossroads of Yiatrakou Str. and Germanikou Str, you will find a small colourful square (Avdis Square), with cafes, bars and a playground.

4.3 ➤ The Peloponnese Railway Station

Starting at Karaiskani Square, take a turn at Diliyianni Str, and you will arrive at this colourful building, built in 1912-1913, with an architectural design combining the neoclassical, central European and Art Nouveau styles. The railway station (serving railway lines to the Peloponnese) is a copy in a reduced scale of the Constantinople railway station, reflecting the European architectural trends of the 19th century. Opposite the Peloponnese Railway Station is the *Larissis Railway Station* (serving railway lines to central and northern Greece), built in 1908, in the neoclassical style, and later reconstructed.

55. The marble fountain at Metaxourgeio Square.

❺ KOLONOS

If you want to go for a walk, you should visit Kolonos, a working-class neighbourhood of Athens, near the historic centre. Although the area has been rebuilt, the neighbourhood maintains its distinct, historic character. Starting at Peloponnese Railway Station take Ioanninon Str, to *Ippiou Kolonou* hill and (take a turn at Evripou Str.) proceed to *Skouze hill.* Around these small wooded hills, you will find an area of detached houses with gardens and small, elegant blocks of flats, preserving the atmosphere of the old Athens neighbourhood (the nearest metro stop is "Sepolia").

39

Tour of Athens, stage 6:

HISTORIC CENTRE (3)
the Philopappou Hill Area

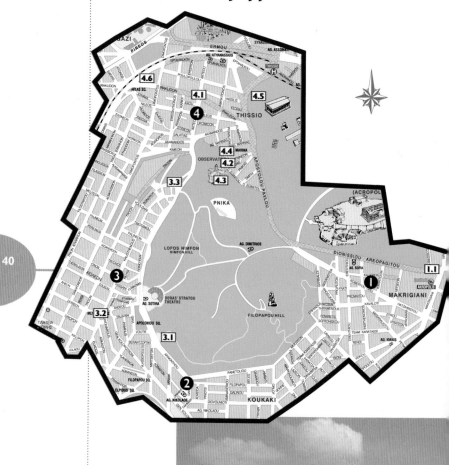

56. A scene of a performance of the "Dora Stratou" theatre. The dance group comprises of 75 dancers, musicians and singers.

❶ MAKRIYIANNI

A residential area, enclosed by the Dionysiou Aeropaghitou Str. to the foothills of Philopappou hill. The neoclassical houses, and the newer buildings, (especially buildings built in the interwar era), are charming.
Makriyianni is one of the most elegant neighbourhoods of the city. Worth a visit are, among others, *Mitsaion Str, Parthenonos Str, Webster Str, Cavalloti Str, R. Gali Str, Mouson Str.*

☞ THE SIGHTS:

1.1 ➤ Acropolis Research Centre
(2-4, Makriyianni Str.)
is a stately building. The building is adorned with Byzantine style masonry with neoclassical decorative motifs. It was built in 1834 by German architect, W. von Weiller. Formerly a military hospital and a base of

police units, it has housed the "Acropolis Research Centre" since 1987. The New Acropolis Museum is being constructed in a nearby space (➥ page 13).

❷ KOYKAKI

Neighbouring Makriyianni is Koukaki, a colourful neighbourhood, especially the area near Philopappou hill *(Panaitoliou Str, Arakinthou Str.).*

❸ ANO PETRALONA

A charming, colourful neighbourhood, exuding the atmosphere of 1950's Athens. Several examples of working-class urban architecture are preserved, among others, one-storey and two storey houses.

☞ THE SIGHTS:

3.1 ➤ Dora Stratou Theatre
is located west of the hill (ancient Amphitheatre). You can see performances of Greek

57. A detail of the plaque of the northern frieze of the Parthenon (Acropolis Museum).

folk dances by the Dora Stratou dance group. Dora Stratou dedicated her life to the research and preservation of Greek folk art. The group, which has participated in a multitude of festivals worldwide, is known in Greece and abroad. The dancers wear traditional Greek costumes of various regions of the country, and perform songs and dances of all periods of Greece's history.

58. Ap. Pavlou Street in the vicinity of the Theseion.

3.2 ➤ Mercouri Square

is a colourful square, with small cafes, and traditional tavernas, in the nearby streets.

3.3 ➤ Stone-built houses

An attractive, small neighbourhood – enclosed by Aginoros Str. and Troon Str. -

with stone-built houses, (of the interwar period), exuding the atmosphere of a mountain village, is being redeveloped.

❹ THESEION

The area was named after the nearby ancient temple (➡ *page 16*). A traditional neighbourhood with a multitude of charming neoclassical houses and public mansions. Have a drink at one of the outdoor cafes at Theseion Square (at Apostolou Pavlou Str.), and enjoy a unique view of the Acropolis and the Ancient Agora area.

59. The dome of the National Observatory, the highest point of Nymphon hill.

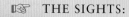 ☞ THE SIGHTS:

4.1 ➤

Irakleidon Str.

is the central pedestrian zone of the area, with attractive neoclassical buildings. Here, and at *Akamantos Str*, which is parallel to Irakleidon Str, you will find a multitude of cafes

and bars, open all day. Moreover, in the nearby pedestrian zone at *Eptahalkou Str.* you will find traditional tavernas with Mediterranean cuisine.

4.2 ➤ **D. Aiginitou Str.**

Connects Apostolou Pavlou Str with the National Observatory. It has a unique view of the Acropolis, Lycabettus hill, the Ancient Agora and the new city.

4.3 ➤ **National Observatory**

The oldest research institution of Greece and the Balkans, was founded in 1842. The building of the Observatory at Nymphon hill, opposite the Acropolis and the Ancient Agora, was designed by Th. Hansen. It is an attractive neoclassical building. The building is cruciform, facing the four compass points.

4.4 ➤ **Ayia Marina Square**

Is a colourful, quiet square, with Ayia Marina church (19th century) at it centre. In the northwestern side, sculpted into the rock, is the original chapel, with a posterior dome and frescoes of the 13th century.

4.5 ➤ **Theseion Park**

is the northwestern section of the Ancient Agora archaeological area. It was planted with trees in 1862 and ornamental plants in 1931. Formerly it was the area where Athenians celebrated Easter.

4.6 ➤ **Poulopoulos Hatfactory** *(66, Iraklidon Str.)*

is a noteworthy industrial building with interesting masonry and a tiled roof. The building, an important landmark that housed a hatfactory many years, is a scheduled building. The space is used for various purposes ("Melina Mercouri" Cultural Centre).

43

▲
60. The popular cafes of Theseion Square offer an unobstructed view of the Ancient Agora and the rock of the Acropolis.

◄
61. The renovated platforms of the Theseion metro station, one of the oldest stations of the network.

Tour of Athens, stage 7:

KOLONAKI
THE RIGILLIS AREA-
METS

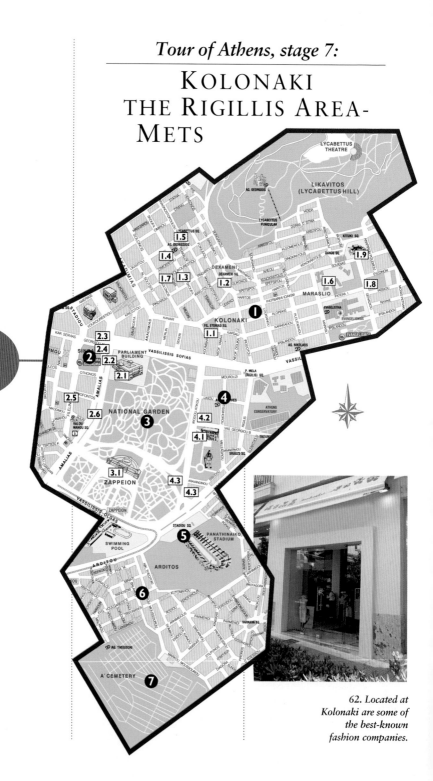

62. Located at
Kolonaki are some of
the best-known
fashion companies.

44

❶ KOLONAKI

Kolonaki is situated at an exclusive location, encompassed by Syntagma Square, and Vassilisis Sofias Avenue. It was named after the old column (the Greek for small column is kolonaki), in the centre of Kolonaki Square. The area was not developed before the 1880's. In Kolonaki you will find parks and attractive buildings, built predominantly in the neoclassical and modernist architectural style, lending the area a distinguished character. It is considered the "aristocratic" neighbourhood of Athens. You will find here the most expensive commercial shops, popular cafes and modern bars, and luxury restaurants. If you seek diversion and relaxation and go for a stroll at *Patriarchou Ioakim Str, Tsakalou Str, Anagnostopoulou Str, Milioni Str, Fokylidou Str, Karneadou Str, Loukianou Str, Ploutarchou Str, Haritos Str, Spefsipou Str. and the Lykabettos circular.*

☞ THE SIGHTS:

1.1 ➤ Kolonaki Square (Philikis Etairias Square)

63. Tsakalof Street, one of the central roads of Kolonaki, with a multitude of cafes and commercial shops, is a busy street.

45

When you visit Athens you should have a coffee at one of the cafes at Kolonaki Square. Modern Athenians and foreign visitors enjoy a break at one of the cafes, eating, drinking coffee and chatting.

1.2 ➤ Dexamenis Square

is a small square, which serves as a local recreation ground. The traditional café on the square attracts Athenians and visitors. It was the meeting place of intellectuals in the 20th century. You will find here an old aqueduct and an outdoor cinema.

1.3 ➤ Skoufa Str.

is the central street of Kolonaki, with interesting neoclassical and art nouveau style buildings. In the section from Kolonaki Square to Delfon Str. are a multitude of shops and modern cafes.

46

▲
64. A view of Kolonaki from the foot of Lycavittos hill. A series of steps lead to the top.

Education of State Education," an attractive neoclassical building (at the crossroads of Marasli Str. and Spefsipou Str.), it is the work of architect D. Kallias (1905).

1.7 ➤ Voukourestiou Str.

distinctive Athens road, it connects the foot of Lycavittos hill with Syntagma Square. In the pedestrian zone (linking Academias Str. to Panepistimiou Str.), you will find a multitude of attractive cafes and bars.

1.8 ➤ Taxiarches
the church of the Petraki Monastery in Kolonaki, ☛ page 24).

1.9 ➤ Gennadios Library
(☛ *page 88*).

1.4 ➤ Ayios Dionysios
(Skoufa Str.)

a stately church, was built in the early 1930's at the site of an earlier church. The façade is built in a neo-renaissance style, and the interior is decorated in the Byzantine style. Ayios Dionysios Areopagitis, one of Athens' early Christians, is the patron saint of Athens.

1.5 ➤ Lycavittos Square

is located near Ayios Dionysios (at the crossroads of Lycavittou Str. and Anagnostopoulou Str.). Dominating the square is the Dragoumis Mansion (1925), a private residence, which formerly accommodated the Brazilian Embassy.

1.6 ➤ Marasleio
The "Marasleio College of

65. A traditional silver bracelet (19th century), from the Eastern Thrace region (Benaki Museum).

Shopping in Kolonaki:
In Kolonaki you will find the most fashionable boutiques, with high couture items produced by Greek and international designers, among others, shoes, and leather goods, toys, old furniture, jewellery, house ware. At Voukourestiou Str. and the surrounding area - in the vicinity of Syntagma Square - you will find world-famous Greek jewellers, bookshops specialising in foreign language editions, and major galleries exhibiting the works of Greek painters and sculptors.

❷ SYNTAGMA SQUARE

Syntagma Square is Athens' central square. The name of the square is derived from an uprising on 3 September 1843, of the people and the guard of Athens before the then Palace building, (what is now the Parliament), demanding that King Otto grant a Constitution. Syntagma Square and Omonia Square are the two central locations of the city. You should not be surprised when you ask directions if people refer to Syntagma square. Plaka, the Acropolis, the Cathedral, the National Garden, Ermou Str, and Kolonaki, are located in the vicinity of Syntagma Square. The most fashionable cafes and small restaurants are located here. The square is busy around the clock. At the kiosks you will find miscellaneous items, among others, aspirins, souvenirs, newspapers, and foreign magazines.

☞ THE SIGHTS:

2.1 ➤ THE PARLIAMENT

Dominating Syntagma Square, the building was the residence of the first king of Greece Otto. The building was constructed from 1836 to 1842. George A', who succeeded Otto on the throne, also resided in the palace. During his reign, two successive fires destroyed the building, making it unsuitable for use as a royal residence. In 1924 the government decided to situate Parliament in the building. Reconstruction work was completed in 1934.

47

66. The building of the Greek Parliament.

67. The monumental space of the "Unknown Soldier".

The interior was redesigned by architect A. Kriezis. In Parliament you will find national treasures, such as the first Greek Constitution, and a multitude of valuable paintings. The library is worth a visit.

2.2 > Monument of the Unknown Soldier

Built from 1929-1932, in front of Parliament, it is a sculpted depiction of a slain soldier (the work of sculptor K. Dimitriades), bearing an inscription with excerpts of Pericle's Epitaph. Commemorated on the marble wall surrounding the monument are the greatest battles of the Greek army posterior to 1821. Greek and visiting officials lay a wreath at the monument on national holidays. The monument is guarded around the clock by two select troops, called Evzones. The ceremony of the changing of the guard, which takes place every hour, is worth seeing.

68. The hotel "Grande Bretagne" dominating the north-eastern side of Syntagma Square.

2.3 > "Grande Bretagne" Hotel

a luxury hotel, built in 1842. The building, designed as a private residence, was the work of Th. Hansen. Renovated in 1874, it accommodated a hotel. In 1958 the hotel was reconstructed to meet increasing demand, and several floors were added to the structure. In 2003 the building was completely renovated. The hotel is connected to major events of Greek history. A multitude of notables and celebrities visiting Athens stayed here. Worth a visit is the interior, with a café and luxury restaurant, exuding a unique atmosphere.

2.4 > Ancient aqueduct

A section of the *ancient cemetery* and *Peisitstratos aqueduct*, unearthed in the northeastern section of the square, is displayed in an outdoor, covered area.

2.5 > Philellinon Str.

is a prolongation of Stadiou Str. You will find here attractive neoclassical buildings and, at the crossroads of Philellinon

48

69. One of a multitude of refreshment stands at the verdant National Garden.

49

Str. Xenophontos Str. and Souri Str. the Sotira Lykodimou church (➡️ *page 22*) and the Anglican church of *Saint Paul* (1843), the work of Ch. Hansen, with elements of Gothic style and cruciform shape.

2.6 ➤ **Amalias Avenue**

is a broad avenue connecting Hadrian's Arch (➡️ *page 7*) with Syntagma Square. An elegant street with stately neoclassical and modernist buildings, it is located in the vicinity of the National Gardens. As you ascend towards Syntagma Square, you will have a view of Parliament and, in the distance, Lycavittos hill.

❸ NATIONAL GARDEN

The National Garden, open from dawn to sunset, is an oasis in the centre of the city. It has a total area of 160,000 m². Some five hundred different kinds of plants, bushes and trees from various locations around the world are grown here. The National Garden – which was formerly the palace garden - was laid out from 1838-1860. There are four entrances: at Vassilisis Sophias Avenue, Herodou Attikou Str, Vassilisis Amalias Avenue, and an entrance connecting the National Garden to the Zappeion. It is a good place to go for a walk, sit on a bench, listen to the singing of the birds and relax. You will also find here a *lake* with ducks, the

70. Zappeion Mansion.

Botanical Museum, a small traditional *café*, a *children's library*, and a *playground*.

3.1 ➤ ZAPPEION MANSION

An attractive building designed by Th. Hansen, it was constructed from 1874-1888. In the past few years some of the most significant events in the history of the country have taken place in the "Conferences and Exhibitions Mansion," such as European summits, the announcement of election results, and significant political announcements. Moreover, art exhibitions and occasionally concerts are held here. In the vicinity of the mansion are the statues of the Zappa brothers, who funded the construction of the

71. The dome of the atrium at Zappeion Mansion.

building, and an attractive park, where Athenians go for a walk, especially on Sundays. Near the Zappeion Mansion is a luxury café and an outdoor cinema.

❹ THE RIGILLIS AREA

A prestigious area with luxury residential buildings, villas and abundant vegetation. It is encompassed by Vassilisis Sophias Avenue, Rigillis Str, Vassileos Konstantinou Avenue and Irodou Attikou Str. The area is located in the vicinity of the old palace (now the Presidential Mansion).

4.1 ➤ Presidential Mansion
(Herodou Attikou Str.)

The former loyal palace was built in the neoclassical and eclectic style (1890-1897) by the architect Ern. Ziller. Formerly it was used as the residence of princes-crown princes, later as a palace, and in 1974 as the official residence of the President of the Hellenic Republic. It has an attractive garden. The mansion is guarded by Evzones, wearing a distinctive uniform.

4.2 ➤ Maximou Mansion
(Herodou Attikou Str.)

the official residence of the respective Greek prime minister, it was designed in 1924 by Ant. Helmes. The mansion was constructed following the death of Helmes, by his wife, and her new husband D. Maximos. It has a small garden.

4.3 ➤
The statues

The sculptures at the junction of Herodou Attikou Str. (facing Kallimarmaro Stadium) are among the most attractive in Athens: the **Discus thrower**, a bronze statue by K. Dimitriades (1927), the **marble Woodchopper** by D. Filippotis, 1872-1875) – gymnast V. Yiannoulis posed for the work – and the **Statue of G. Karaiskakis**, a bronze monumental sculpture (4.40 metres high), by M. Tombros (1963-1966), depicting a hero of the Greek revolution on horseback.

72. The "Xylothrafstis" ("woodchopper") one of the distinctive statues of Athens.

51

73. The Presidential Mansion, at Herodou Attikou Street.

74. The Panathenaikon (Kallimarmaro) Stadium.

52

75. One of the distinctive "Hermes" statues facing the track of the Panathenaikon Stadium. One faces the grandstand and the other faces the track.

❺ PANATHENAIKON (KALLIMARMARO) STADIUM

The Panathenaikon stadium, a remarkable construction, was made of white marble. The petal shaped stadium is located facing the National Garden. In 330 BBC a stadium made of wood was built at this location. Herodes Atticus constructed a marble construction, which was the model for the construction of the stadium that stands today.

It was used as a space for athletic competitions, which took place during the Panathenaean festival. The stadium that stands today was built in 1869-1870 for the first Olympic Games in modern history (1896). Surrounding the stadium is the wooded *Ardittou hill*, where local residents go for a walk.

❻ METS

The most fashionable neighbourhood of Athens, was developed in the 1870's. It was named after the Mets brewery that was located in the area, and decades it was a popular recreational area. In the 1950's the riverbed of the *Ilissos river* (at Ardittou Str.) passed through it. Today it is a quiet residential area, encompassed by the Ardittou hill and the 1st Cemetery (along the *Loginou Str.* pedestrian zone). In the central road of the area, M. Mousourou Str, are cafes. Worth seeing are other distinctive roads of the neighbourhood (among others, *Nik. Theotokis Str, Trivonianou Str, Dikaiarchou Str, Balanou Str.*). If you take *Kleitomachou Str, Archimidou Str.* and *Embedokleous Str*, you will reach **Varnava square.** You will find here cafes, traditional tavernas and luxury restaurants. You can return to the Panathenaikion Stadium via Agras Str.

❼ 1st CEMETERY

It is the oldest and biggest cemetery of Athens. Several important personalities of modern Greece have been laid to rest here (among others, politicians, scientists and artists). The foundation of the cemetery coincided with the foundation of the modern Greek state. The design recalls the major cemeteries of Western Europe in the early 1900's. It is basically an outdoor sculpture display, with a stately and serene garden, excellent monumental tombstones, built by some of the most important Greek sculptors of the past two centuries.

☞ THE SIGHTS:

The Sleeping Maiden ("Koimomeni"): The most famous sculpture of modern Greek art, made by G. Halepas in 1878, for the grave of S. Afentakis.

G. Averof Monument: The grandest monument of the cemetery, built by the sculptors G. Vitalis, and D. Filippotis. The remains of the national benefactor are here.

Er. Schlieman Monument: The tomb monument of the German archaeologist who discovered ancient Troy, made by Ern. Ziller (1892). It is shaped like a church. On the groundwork are sculpted depictions of the Trojan Cycle.

Chr. Zografou Monument: Built in the renaissance style, it recalls the Mausoleum of Lavrenti Medici in Florence.

Nude Angel: A remarkable tombstone sculpture by G. Vitsaris, (1872), on the tomb of N. Koumelis.

76. The famous "Koimomeni" by G. Halepas (1st Cemetery).

Tour of Athens, stage 8:

FROM LYCAVITTOS HILL TO STREFI HILL

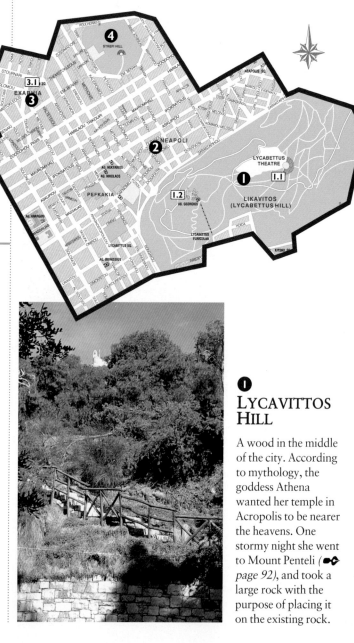

77. Walking on the footpaths of Lycavittos hill is a pleasure.

❶ LYCAVITTOS HILL

A wood in the middle of the city. According to mythology, the goddess Athena wanted her temple in Acropolis to be nearer the heavens. One stormy night she went to Mount Penteli (●✦ *page 92)*, and took a large rock with the purpose of placing it on the existing rock.

78. The view of the city and the Acropolis from the top of Lycavittos hill is unique!

55

As she transported the rock, two black birds approached her, bringing her bad news regarding something she had to take care of immediately. In her rage and haste, the rock fell in the centre of Athens. The rock, which is 278 metres high, is located in the centre of Athens. The Athenians pay tribute to the protecting goddess of their city every time they go there. Lycavittos hill is a special place!

☞ THE SIGHTS:

The view of the city: Don't miss the view of the Acropolis, the whole city and beyond that the sea. Lycavittos is the favourite place of incurable romantics. You will enjoy the view, the pine trees, the Cyprus trees, the small wooden benches and narrow paths. In antiquity the hill was wooded. At the top was a temple dedicated to Zeus. When Athens was liberated, following the revolution against Turkish rule, Lyca-vittos was bare. The refore-station began in 1880 and was completed in 1915.

79. Lycavittos Theatre.

1.1 ➤ **Lycavittos Theatre**

An open-air theatre built from 1964-11965 by the architect T. Zenetos at the site of an old mine following the recommen-dation of the Greek actress A. Synodinou, for performances of ancient drama. It has a capacity of 3,000. In summer cultural events are staged here, attracting music and theatre fans.

1.2 ➤ **Ayios Georgios**
(●◆ page 24)

DIRECTIONS: If you want to go by car, there is only one road leading to the top of the hill. If you want to walk there are a multitude of footpaths. You may also use the funicular,

which operates daily from the crossroads of *Aristippou Str. and Ploutarchou Str.* (Kolonaki).

❷ NEAPOLI

Neapoli is encompassed by Lycavittos hill and Mavromihali Str. It is, after Plaka, the oldest neighbourhood of Athens (Neapolis means New Town). Neapoli and Exharhia were developed in 1860. The first residents were mostly students. The area is situated near the University and the Polytechnic. Later it became a favourite residential neigh-bourhood of artists. At Askli-piou is the remarkable neoclas-sical church of **Ayios Nikolaos Pefkakion** (1895). Facing Lycavittos hill, is an area on a steep incline, with pedestrian zone, lined with trees and steps leading to the central roads (among others, *Solonos Str, Asklipiou Str, Ippokratous Str, Sina Str, Massalias Str,* and *Delfon Str.*) where you will find, among others, a multitude of cafes, small bookshops, antique shops.

❸ EXARHIA

An old Athens neighbourhood, with a special charm. It is known as a residential neighbourhood of students and artists, with a Bohemian character, contrasting with the "worldly" Kolonaki Square. In the past few decades, a series of reconstruction works have considerably upgraded the area. A multitude of

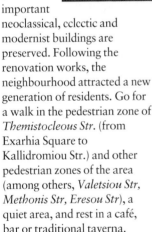

important neoclassical, eclectic and modernist buildings are preserved. Following the renovation works, the neighbourhood attracted a new generation of residents. Go for a walk in the pedestrian zone of *Themistocleous Str.* (from Exarhia Square to Kallidromiou Str.) and other pedestrian zones of the area (among others, *Valetsiou Str, Methonis Str, Eresou Str*), a quiet area, and rest in a café, bar or traditional taverna.

multitude of cafes and small, fashionable bars and two outdoor cinemas, offering unique entertainment in the summer.

❹ STREFI HILL

Strefi hill is located in the vicinity of Exarhia Square. The small hill is a wooded oasis in the densely built city. Here you will find sports facilities, a summer theatre made of stone, and at the top you may enjoy a panoramic view of the city. To get there, you take *Kallidromiou Str*, a beautiful street, with neoclassical mansions and small popular cafes and bars, (from Emm. Benaki Str. to Deliyianni Str.).

80. A detail of the balcony of a neo-classical house in Exarhia.

57

81. Exarhia Square.

☞ THE SIGHTS:

3.1 ▷ Exarhia Square
is the central square of the neighbourhood. It is a busy square, especially in the evening. You will find here a

Tour of Athens, stage 9:

FROM SYNTAGMA SQUARE TO OMONIA SQUARE

❶ SYNTAGMA SQUARE
(➤ page 47)

❷ PANEPISTIMIOU AVENUE
(EL. VENIZELOU)

O ne of the oldest roads of Athens, it was originally designed to be a Boulevard (formerly called Boulevard Str). Today it is one of the busiest roads, linking Syntagma Square with Omonia Square. On this broad avenue, a number of the most important, representative public buildings of Athens were built, unique landmarks of the city.

☞ **THE SIGHTS:**

2.1 ➤ Army Pension Funds Building

A stately building occupying the block encompassed by Panepistimiou Str, Voukourestiou Str, Amerikis Str. and Stadiou Str, it was built from 1927-1938. The royal stables were formerly located here. The façade was built in the Art Deco style. In the centre is an arcade with shops. Recently reconstructed, the building is now a shopping centre and an office building.

2.2 ➤ Iliou Melathron
(12, Panepistimiou Str.)
is one of the most attractive neoclassical buildings of Athens. It was reconstructed in 1879 by Ern. Ziller in the neorennaissance style. It was the residence of the German archaeologist and philhelene Er. Schliemann. It has a double stairway in the northern side, while in the façade and the

82. Iliou Melathron, also known as "Schliemann Mansion".

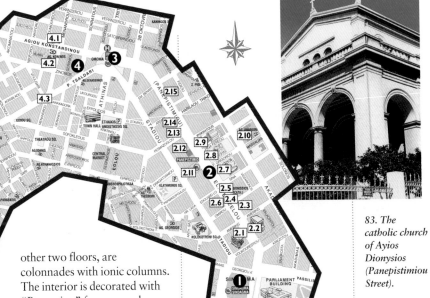

83. The catholic church of Ayios Dionysios (Panepistimiou Street).

59

other two floors, are colonnades with ionic columns. The interior is decorated with "Pompeian" frescoes and depictions of the landscapes and finds of Troy. In 1927 it became the seat of the Supreme Court (the highest penal court of the country). It is now the Numismatic Museum (➥ page 83).

2.3 ➤ Archaeological Society Mansion

A five-storey building, it is an exceptional example of late classicism. The entrance is decorated with ionic columns. Located at the crossroads of Omirou Str. and Panepistimiou Avenue, it houses the Archaeological Society of Athens.

2.4 ➤ Catholic Church of St Dionysos (1853-1865). *(Panepistimiou Avenue and Omirou Str.)*

The three columned, cross-in-square style church was designed by the architects L. von Klenze and L. Kaftantzoglou. The portico in the western side has five cylindrical arches.

2.5 ➤ Athens Eye-Clinic *(Panepistimiou Avenue and Sina Str.)*

A stately building (1854) with elements of Byzantine and neoclassical architecture, it was designed by Ch. Hansen and modified by L. Kaftantzoglou. Formerly a one-storey building, in the mid-1860's a second floor was added to the structure.

◄

84. A detail of the central entrance of the Athens Eye-Clinic.

85. The stately building of the Academy of Athens.

2.6 ⮞ Bank of Greece Mansion
(21 Panepistimiou Str.)

A stately building occupying a whole block. The foundations were laid in 1933 and the building was opened in 1938. The transactions halls recall the unadorned, stately atmosphere of the interwar period.

The three temples of learning
("the athenian triad")

Three buildings constructed by two Danish architects, the Hansen brothers, who lived in Greece.

2.7 ⮞ *Academy (1859-1887):* On either side of the

86. Over the central entrance of the Athens University (see right) are the frescoes of the Bavarian K. Rahl (see left).

Academy, are two wings decorated with friezes and a pair of high columns supporting the statues of Apollo and Athena. The Academy was studied by Th. Hansen, the younger of the Hansen brothers. The statues were sculpted by L. Drosis and the painted decoration was produced by K. Rahl. The Aca-

demy is thought to be a prime example of Greek architectural style..

2.8 ➤ *University (1839-1864):* The Athens University was designed by Ch. Hansen the elder of the brothers Hansen. Worth seeing are the fountain in the court, the circular stairway and the multicoloured frescoes with classical themes (designed by the Bavarian K. Rahl), decorating the walls, located behind the columns on the balcony.

2.9 ➤ *National Library (1887-1902):* A remarkable building, planned by Th. Hansen. It is the largest library in the country, housing a unique range of thousands of books in all languages. On the façade is a stately six-column portico in the Doric style, based on the design of the Theseion. The interior, designed by Ern. Ziller, is lighted by a skylight on the roof and encompassed by an Ionian style colonnade.

87. *The construction of the National Library was funded by P. Vallianos. In the foreground the statue of the donor.*

61

88. *The Statue of Apollo at the top of a Ionian style column, at the entrance of the Athens Academy.*

89. *The propylaea of the Athens University.*

2.10 ➤ Cultural Centre of the Municipality of Athens

Located in the vicinity of the "triad" *(at 50, Akademias Str.)*, it is a remarkable neoclassical building. It was built in 1835 according to the design of Chr. Hansen. It was a hospital in the course of decades. Cultural events are held in the building. In front of the main entrance of the building is a small garden with the busts of historical figures (among others, artists and politicians), while on the other side, (at Solonos Str.), is a traditional café. Exactly adjacent to the café (at Akademias Str.) is the stately **Palamas building** (with a pink interior, it is known as the "pink building"). Built in 1857-1859, it houses the *Theatrical Museum* library. Diagonally across the street, (at the crossroads of Ippocratous Str.

and Massalias Str.), is the **Student Union of the University of Athens** (1926-1931), designed by Al. Nikoloudis in the eclectic style of the Beaux Arts.

2.11 ➤ Korai Square

is a small, attractive square, developed when a pedestrian street was created at Korai Str. North-east of the square is the **Rallis building** (10, Korai Square) built in the early neoclassical style. Opposite the Rallis building is the modernist building of the **General Accounting Office** (designed by E. Lazaridis). Northwest of the square is the remarkable former hotel **Grand Hotel** (2, Korai Square). Opposite the Grand Hotel is the modern building of the **Commercial Bank**. At the square you will also find the recently renovated **"Athens Arcade"** with a multitude of cafes, fast food restaurants, shops, and a cinema.

2.12 ➤ Ionian Bank Mansion
(Pesmatzoglou Str.)

A remarkable eclectic style mansion with art deco decoration (1925). The central transactions hall has a notable colonnade and balconies. The lighting, a skylight with stained glass windows, is spectacular.

2.13 ➤ Arsakeion Mansion (1846-1955)

A stately two-storey mansion, it is a distinctive example of Greek classicism with a strain of eclecticism. Formerly the Arsakeion Girls School, it is now the Council of State, (highest Court of State). Adjacent to the mansion is the Courts Square.

90. The Cultural Centre of Athens Municipality and its small garden.

2.14 ➤ *Arsakeion Arcade (Orpheos):* The arcade in the Mansion, built in the neobaroque style, has a remarkable glass roof with a dome in the centre. You will find here shops, cafes and the *"Stoa tou Vivliou"* (Book Arcade) with the bookshops of 60 Greek publishers. Cultural events are held at the Stoa tou Vivliou.

2.15 ➤ **"Rex"** Cinema

A mansion with three halls (cinema-theatre), built from 1935-1937, the design was influenced by contemporary American skyscrapers. Two halls are now used for performances of the National Theatre. The third is an entertainment centre.

❸ OMONIA SQUARE

A central square, which is busy around the clock, throughout the year, by contrast with Syntagma Square. Omonia Square has always been busy around the clock. According to custom, Athenians, after a night out Saturday evening, buy Sunday papers art kiosks and stands on the square. Omonia is the oldest central square of modern Athens. A visit to Omonia, to get a sense of the vibrancy of the square is a must for all visitors. At the square you will find the usual fast-food shops. Foreign newspapers are sold in kiosks. At the square are stately buildings, in particular the hotels **"Bangeion"** and **"Alexandros"** *(at the crossroads of Athinas Str.),* the **"Neon"** café, and a branch of the **National Bank** *(at Panepistimiou Str.).*

91. Two silver domes decorating the tower-like corners of the Arsakeio Megaro facing Stadiou Street.
◄

92. A view of Omonia Square with buildings of a variety of architectural styles.
▼

63

93. Panepistimiou Avenue by night, at the junction with Omonia Square.

❹ THE OMONIA SQUARE AREA

Stadiou Str, Patision Str, Panepistimiou Avenue, 3rd Septemvriou Str, Piraeus Str, Athinas Str. and Ayiou Konstantinou Str. converge at Omonia Square. It is a lively area, with interesting places (small shops, traditional cafes etc.). At Omonia Square is a central metro station

☞ THE SIGHTS:

4.1 ➤ THE NATIONAL THEATRE OF GREECE
(Ayiou Konstantinou Str.)

Built from 1891-1901, according to the design of Ern. Ziller, it was commissioned by the king George I and funded by Greeks residing abroad. A replica of the National Theatre of Vienna, it is built in the renaissance style. The theatre opened in November 1901. It was formerly called the Royal Theatre, but in 1930 it was renamed National Theatre. The central auditorium (Italian style) has a capacity of 1000 (stalls, dress circle, upper circle, and two boxes). Facing the theatre *(at Menandrou Str.)* is the three-storey neoclassical **Eynar Mansion**, which accommodates a Museum dedicated to actors K. Paxinou and A. Minotis.

4.2 ➤ AYIOS KONSTANTINOS
(Ayiou Konstantinou Str.)

Facing the National Theatre, it is a monumental church (1871-1896/1905) built by L. Kaftan-tzoglou. The recently renovated three-columned, cross-in-square church has an stately façade in a combination of neoclassical and renaissance styles, a monumental entrance in the form of an ancient propylaea, and an attractive interior decoration.

4.3 ➤ PIRAEUS STR.
(P. Tsaldari Str.)

Constructed along the path of the ancient road uniting Athens with Piraeus. The Long Walls were constructed along the side of the street. The first paved road in Athens, Piraeus Str. links the city with the port of Piraeus. In the 19th century an industrial zone was developed and a multitude of factories were constructed along the road. In the past few years a multitude of factories were renovated and used for another purpose (museums, cultural centres, the Higher School of Fine Arts). The buildings at Piraeus Str, a very busy street, are interesting examples of industrial architecture.

4.4 ➤ Koumoundourou Square (Eleftherias)

An attractive, wooded square. Facing Piraeus Square is the grand neoclassical mansion of the **"Municipal Gallery"** built in 1874 (designed by G. Metaxas). Neighbouring the gallery is the small church of **Ayioi Anargyroi** (1893). Located on the square is a small stone-built theatre, which is used for events.

4.5 ➤ Ayioi Asomatoi Str.

As you descend Piraeus Str. take a left turn at Ayioi Asomatoi Str. You will find at number 45 one of the best-known traditional buildings of Athens (picturesque classicist style, 1880), with copies of the famous twin Caryatids on the balcony. The house, is among the most photographed and painted themes of Athens.

4.6 ➤ *Gazi*
(✆ page 38)

4.7 ➤ Botanical Gardens of the University of Athens

Located at the crossroads of *Iera Odos* (Iera Odos in Greek means Sacred Road) (built along the path of the ancient road of the Eleusinian Mysteries) and *Sp. Patsi Str.* It has a total area of 7,000 m2. Some 120 varieties of trees and plants and mosses and grasses from different parts of the world.

94. Copies of the Caryatids, at the small house at Ayion Asomaton Street 45.
◀

65

95. The Botanical Garden of the Athens University.

Tour of Athens, stage 10:

FROM OMONIA SQUARE
TO KYPSELI

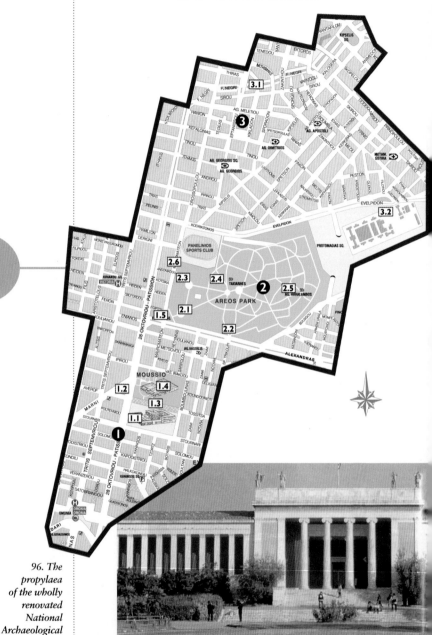

96. The propylaea of the wholly renovated National Archaeological Museum.

❶ PATISION STR
(28th OCTOVRIOU STR)

A central road linking Patisia to the centre, before the early 20th century Patision Str. was a rural area with small houses and gardens! Following rapid development, it became clearly an urban location, now one of the busiest streets of Athens. Among a multitude of new buildings, neoclassical, Art Nouveau and modernist buildings are preserved. As you head from the crossroads of Patision Str and Alexandras Avenue towards Patisia, on your left is *Victorias Square* (at 3rd Septemvriou Str.), on your right is the stately *Higher School of Economic and Scientific Studies*, (1935), on your left the *"Hara"* block of flats, an pioneering work built in the 1920's at Patision Str. 337 and on your right the *Kypriadis neighbourhood* (in the vicinity of Papadiamantis Square), formerly a garden city (with villas, two-storey blocks of flats, densely vegetated) developed in the 1920's - the suburban style has been preserved notwithstanding subsequent development.

☞ THE SIGHTS:

1.1 ➤ Polytechnic (National Metsovio Polytechnic)

Designed by the architect L. Kaftantzoglou, the Polytechnic was built from 1861-1876. It is an archetype of the urban tradition of Athens. It comprises of a central building and T-shaped wings facing Patision Str. It has two floors and the entrance is elevated. Tow monumental staircases lead to the Ionian style four-column propylaea of the ground floor, a copy of the northern hall of the Erechtheion (●◆ *page 12*).

1.2 ➤ "Acropol Palace" Hotel (1925-1926).

A five-story building designed by the architect I. Mayiasis, the Acropol Palace is a distinctive example of Athens Art Nouveau architecture.

1.3 ➤ Tositsa Str.

A wide pedestrian zone, flanked by the National Metsovio Polytechnic and the garden of the National Archaeological Museum, with a row of trees in the middle, Tositsa Str. is a place to relax and stroll.

97. *Bell-shaped idol with movable legs from Thebes, Boeotia (early 7th century B.C.), a model of the mascot of the Athens 2004 Olympic Games. (In the photo an exact copy of the idol. You may purchase one at the shops of the Archaeological Resources Fund.)*

98. Pedion tou Areos: the statue of Athena Promahou at the southern entrance of the park (Alexandras Avenue).

1.4 ▷ National Archaeological Museum

A stately building constructed in the late 19th century, the National Archaeological Museum was designed by L. Lange and Ern. Ziller. The Ionian style propylaea are adorned with clay statues, the copies of ancient works, while on either side is an oblong arcade. Athenians like to stroll in the attractive garden in front of the museum, especially in summer *(for museum exhibits ●◀ page 80)*.

1.5 ▷ Egyptou Square

An elegant square with neoclassical and modernist buildings, examples of the formerly bourgeois character of the area, located at the crossroads of Alexandras Avenue, and Patision Str.

❷ PEDION TOU AREOS

Pedion tou Areos, the largest park in Athens (230,000 m²), was laid out in 1934. Named after the roman campus martius, the park used to be a training ground for military units. Athenians like to go for a walk here all year round, or seek entertainment at cafes, outdoor theatres, and other venues.

2.4 ▷ Taxiarhon Church

Post-Byzantine church of the 16th or 17th century. In the court of a monument with the remains and the statue of prince Alexander Ypsilantis (1792-1828), which is closely connected to the Revolution of 1821.

☞ THE SIGHTS:

99. A statue of king Constantine on horseback.

2.1 ▷ *The statue of King Constantine:* A bronze statue of king Constantine (1868-1922) placed on a monumental marble pedestal, erected in 1938. It is located at the central entrance of the park, facing Egyptou Square.

2.2 ▷ *Statue of Athena (Promahou):* A monument dedicated to the British, Australian and New Zealand soldiers killed in the Second World War, it was sculpted in 1952 by sculptor V. Falireas. The marble lioness at the base was sculpted by Ath. Limnaios.

2.3 ▷ *Iroon Avenue:* A wide, stately road in the park with the busts of the freedom fighters of the Greek Revolution. You will find it at the Mavromateon Str. entrance.

2.5 ➤ Ayios Haralambos

The church was built in 1928, in cruciform shape, at the site of an old church. In the church are icons of the important Greek painter F. Kontologou.

2.6 ➤ Mavromateon Str.

An elegant road linking the Archaeological Museum with Kodringtonos Str. Facing Areos Park is a row of stately, luxury blocks of flats, most of them built in 1925-1960, when the street was thought to be the most prestigious location of the city.

❸ KYPSELI

A distinctive bourgeois neighbourhood of Athens, Kypseli has preserved its aristocratic character, although in the past few decades it has been rebuilt and is now densely populated. In the 1990's a multitude of immigrants settled in Kypseli, transforming it into a charming multicultural neighbourhood. Among the modern blocks of flats several examples of stately neoclassical buildings and blocks of flats of the interwar period are preserved, which are worth seeing. They are located on distinctive roads of the neighbourhood (among others, *Drosopoulou Str, Eptanisou Str, Ithakis Str, Tinou Str, Tenedou Str, Spetson Str, Lefkadas Str.*). You will also find in Kypseli the notable churches Ayia Zoni (1927) and Ayios Georgios (Kypselis square, 1931).

☞ THE SIGHTS:

3.1 ➤ Fokionos Negri Str.

A wide, stately, densely vegetated pedestrian zone linking Kypselis Square with Drosopoulou Str, Fokionos Negri Str is the centre of the neighbourhood. Originally called the "green boulevard", Fokionos Negri Str. was built in 1937, at the site of a stream. In the 1960's it acquired a reputation for nightlife, attracting politicians and artists. A busy street throughout the day, it is a popular recreational area, with dozens of cafes, restaurants and small bars.

3.2 ➤ Courts (former Army Cadet School)

A complex of neoclassical buildings, the courts are located south of Kypseli *(Evelpidon Str)*. The building was built from 1900-1904, (designed by Ern. Ziller), for the Army Cadet School. In the early 1980's the Athens Courts were accommodated here.

100. The distinctive Kypseli neighbourhood has been largely redeveloped. However, a multitude of examples of its varied architecture are preserved. ▼

69

Tour of Athens, stage 11:

HISTORICAL WALK

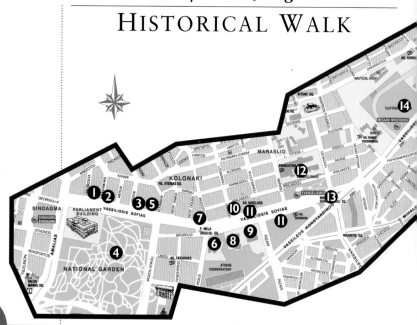

*I*f you don't have much time, in the historical walk *(approximately 3.5 kilometres) you can visit and see the most important monuments and sights of Athens. It is a walk through history, from classical antiquity, through all the historical periods, architectural styles, and successive phases of the development of the city to the 21st century (classical period, roman period, Byzantium, Turkish occupation, neoclassicism, and 20th century). In fact it is a walk in history, which only Athens can offer.*

ACROPOLIS *(●◆ page 10)*

ODEION OF HERODES ATTICUS *(●◆ page 9)*

PLAKA *(●◆ page 26)*

BYZANTINE MONUMENTS IN ATHENS *(●◆ page 20)*

OTTOMAN MONUMENTS IN ATHENS *(●◆ page 25)*

SYNTAGMA SQUARE *(●◆ page 47)*

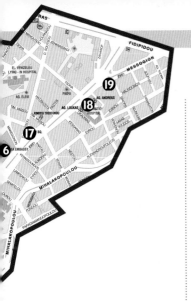

VASSILISIS SOPHIAS AVENUE

The most impressive road of Athens, linking Syntagma Square to Ampelokoipoi. Formerly called Kifisias Avenue, it linked Athens to the traditional suburb of Kifisia. It has in part lost the original character of a classic boulevard. However, it is one the most charming roads of the city, with some of the most attractive buildings, museums and parks.

SIGHTS (from Syntagma Square to Ampelokoipoi):

❶ THE GREEK MINISTRY OF FOREIGN AFFAIRS BUILDING
(5, Vassilisis Sophias Avenue)

The work of Ern. Ziller (1872-1873), it belonged to the Syngrou family before being bequeathed to the Greek state in 1921. The neoclassical mansion housing the main services of the ministry, has been designated a work of art. In 1985 it was linked to a later building, at *Zalokosta Str.*

❷ FRENCH EMBASSY
(Psyha Mansion)

A stately three-storey building at the crossroads of Akademias Str.). It was built in 1894 by An. Metaxas for the Psyha family. It has notable modernist decorative elements connected to the neoclassical style.

❸ THE ITALIAN EMBASSY

The residence of prince Nicholas, before the expulsion of the royal family in 1917, it later accommodated a luxury hotel ("Le Petit Palais"). Later it was bought by the Italian government to accommodate the embassy.

❹ THE NATIONAL GARDEN
(➥ page 49)

71

◄
101. A detail of the central building of the Greek Ministry of Foreign Affairs.

72

▲
102. The Benaki Museum mansion.

❼ THE STATHATOS MANSION

A remarkable neoclassical mansion *(at the crossroads of Irodotou Str. and Vassilisis Sophias Avenue)*, Stathatos Mansion was designed by E. Ziller in 1885. It accommodates the new wing of the Goulandris Museum of Cycladic and Ancient Greek Art (●● *page 83)*. It is linked to the museum by a glass-covered passage.

❽ THE BYZANTINE AND CHRISTIAN MUSEUM

The main building of the Museum is "Villa Ilisia"(1848), a neorenaissance style building, constructed at the bank of the then uncovered Ilissos river. It was the residence of S. de Marbois-Lebrun, known as the "Duchess of Placentia." The building was designed by St. Kleanthes, (or according to some sources Chr. Hansen). Following the death of the duchess (1854), the mansion was acquired by the Greek state. It has accommodated the museum since 1930. Two new wings were built in 1952 and 1994 *(for exhibits* ●● *page 85)*.

❺ THE BENAKI MUSEUM
(1, Koumpari Str.)

The most impressive neoclassical building of Athens, it was built in stages from 1910 to 1931 (designed by An. Metaxas). Formerly the residence of Ant. Benakis, since 1931 it houses the Museum exhibits (●● *page 84)*.

❻ THE SAROGLEIO MANSION
(Officers Club)

A stately building constructed in the Beaux Arts style, it is located at Rigillis Square (P. Mella). It was designed by architect Al. Nikoloudis.

103. The Stathatos Mansion.

⑨ THE WAR MUSEUM

A modern building (designed by Th. Valentis), constructed in 1975 (☞ *page 86*).

THE RESIDENCE OF ⑩ THE BRITISH AMBASSADOR

Located at the crossroads of Vassilisis Avenue and Loukianou Str, the building was constructed from 1930-1932 (designed by An. Metaxas). Formerly the residence of then Prime Minister Eleftherios Venizelos, it was granted to the British state following his death. It accommodated the British embassy in Athens before 1960. Following the construction in a neighbouring location of the new building of the embassy, it became the residence of the ambassador.

⑪ AYIOS NIKOLAOS and AYIOS GEORGIOS

Small churches in cruciform four-column style, Ayios Nikolaos and Ayios Georgios are representative examples of the architectural currents of the late 19th century. *Ayios Nikolaos* (1876 neighbouring the British embassy) is built in a distinctive neo-Byzantine style, while *Ayios Georgios* combines the Byzantine, classicist and roman styles.

73

▲
104. A view of Vassilisis Sophias Avenue with the War Museum and a section of Rizari park.

105. Rizari park.

106. The "Dromeas" at Megali tou Genous Scholi Square (Vassilisis Sophias Avenue).

74

⑫ THE EVANGELISMOS HOSPITAL
(old building)

A neoclassical building (designed by G. Metaxas) Evangelismos hospital was inaugurated in 1880 by then Queen Olga. Later an English-style garden was laid out in the yard.

⑬ MEGALIS TOU GENOUS SCHOLI SQUARE

A small square at the crossroads of Vassilisis Sophias Avenue and Vassileos Konstantinou Avenue. In the centre is the impressionist sculpture of K. Varotsos **"Dromeas"** (1988), sculpted exclusively out of sheets of glass. Facing the square is the **"Hilton"** hotel, with elements of the international modernist style (at the neighbouring streets, Ventiri Str, Mexi Str. etc. are cafes, bars and small restaurants). On the opposite side of the square (at the crossroads of Vassilisis Sofias Avenue and Gennadiou Str.) are two remarkable art nouveau blocks of flats of the interwar period. Adjacent to the **"Hilton"** hotel is the building of the **National Gallery-Alexandros Soutzos Museum** (●◆ *page 86*), built in 1966-1975 in the brutalist architectural style of Le Corbusier. Facing the National Gallery is the ***Rizari park***, one of Athens' oldest gardens.

⑭ ELEFTHERIAS PARK

A park with a statue of Eleftherios Venizelos (sculpted by the sculptor G. Pappas). In the rear section are three stone built buildings, accommodating the **Athens Municipality Arts Centre** and the **"Eleftherios Venizelos Museum"**. Facing the part is a row of three unadorned neoclassical buildings of the hospitals "Aeghinitio", Aretaeio", and "Alexandra".

107. The "Hilton" hotel.

⓯ THE ATHENS CONCERT HALL

A monumental work (designed by M. Vourekas), the Athens Concert Hall was built in stages from 1973-1991. It is thought to be one of the best concert halls in the world. It has, among others, concert and opera halls, a musical library, a conference centre, and halls for multiple uses. In the winter concerts, opera, theatre and dance performances, and other events, are held here.

⓰ THE AMERICAN EMBASSY

One of the most important example of modern architecture in Athens (1959-1961), designed by the famous architect W. Gropius.

⓱ MAVILI SQUARE

Among the most "vibrant" squares of Athens, with a multitude of cafes, bars and restaurants in the area, Mavili Square attracts visitors throughout the day. It is a prestigious residential area, near Lycavittos hill and the central Vassilisis Sophias Avenue and Alexandras Avenue. Recently it has lost some of its former charm as a result of the traffic on the surrounding streets.

⓲ THE IPPOKRATEIO HOSPITAL

A scheduled public building, constructed in the 1880's in the neoclassical style. It has accommodated a hospital since 1912. Adjacent to the hospital is the chapel of *Ayios Andreas* (17th century).

⓳ TOWER OF ATHENS

The first glass skyscraper of Athens (1971-1973) – one of a few skyscrapers constructed in the greater urban area of the capital. A complex of respectively two 25- and 12- storey buildings, the tower of Athens accommodates mainly company offices. In front of the Tower of Athens is a small villa with a garden, a relic of the 1920's when the area (Ampelokoipoi) was rural.

108. The Tower of Athens, at the crossroads of Vassilisis Sophias Avenue and Mesogheion Avenue.
▼

SUBURBS

During your stay in Athens you may want to visit the suburbs. In the suburbs you may go for a walk on vegetated roads, and relax at a confectionery or café.

THE NORTHERN SUBURBS
(Psihiko, Filothei, Maroussi, Kifisia).

▲
109. Old eclectic building in Kifisia. The building houses a modern shopping centre.

The suburbs of **Psihiko**, and **Filothei** were developed in the late 1920's on the model of British garden cities. They are quiet residential areas, with attractive villas, abundant vegetation and broad streets.

In **Maroussi** are the facilities of the *Olympic Athletic Centre of Athens (O.A.K.A.)*.

Kifisia is perhaps the most elegant suburb of northern Athens. The luxury villas of Kifisia of the 19th century were raised by the oldest Athenian families. With attractive villas and vibrant shopping streets, and the branches of Greek and

110. An impressive mansion of Kifisia.

foreign shops, Kifisia is an attractive area. Worth seeing is the *Goulandri Natural History Museum (●❖ page 89)*, open air cinemas and the Flower Show, which takes place every year in Kifisia grove. Some of the best restaurants, confectioneries and cafes of Athens are in Kifisia.

Alsos Syngrou, (1,000,000 m^2)

adjacent to Kifisia and Maroussi, a wooded area, is an ideal place to go for a walk and relax.

The main road linking Athens to the suburbs is Kifisias Avenue. You can reach Maroussi and Kifisia on line 1 of the metro.

77

111. The Athens Olympic Stadium (see right), location of a multitude of athletic installations and recreation areas, linked to other areas of the capital by bus lines, the suburban railway and the metro (see left). The roof was designed by the well-known architect S. Calatrava.

112. A distinctive circular building in the "Floisvos" neighbourhood of P. Faliro.

THE SOUTHERN SUBURBS
(Faliro, Glyfada, Voula, Vouliagmeni, Varkiza)

The southern suburbs are located on the coast of the Saronic Gulf, from Piraeus to cape Vouliagmeni. Access from Athens is easy (the southern suburbs are just 20-30 minutes from the centre). The southern suburbs are an ideal place to go for a walk by the seaside, and swim. The best and most popular beaches of Attica, with clean water (➥ *page 117)* are located here. The areas each have a shopping centre with superb shops. In the southern suburbs you can walk on the marinas, have lunch or dinner by the seaside, enjoy your favourite water sports, and play golf.

The *Glyfada Golf Club* is open daily from 08:00 am to sunset. Situated along the coast are hotels with a view of the sea.

In the coastal area of the **bay of Faliro**, (from Neo Faliro to Paleo Faliro) is a huge recreational and cultural park with facilities for cultural events, a remarkable aquarium putting on display the submarine species of the seas of Greece and the Mediterranean, a birds garden, nautical facilities, and an *esplanade* with small refreshment bars. In **Trocadero (P. Faliro)** you may visit the Nautical Museum, on one of the most famous warships of

113. View of Glyfada from the sea.

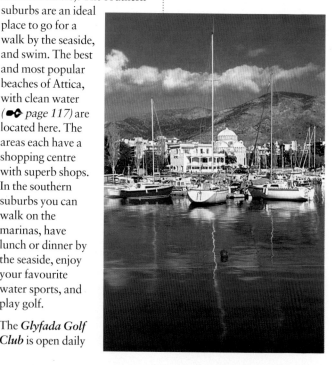

114.
Vouliagmeni
lake has
therapeutic
water.
The geological
attraction is
the popular
destination
of the residents
of Attica.

recent Greek history, the battleship Averof. In **Ayios Kosmas** is a large seaside park. A metropolitan park with an area of 4,000,000 m2 will be constructed in the area of the old airport **(Helleniko)**.

Vouliagmeni is an attractive suburb with abundant vegetation, elegant villas, attractive beaches, the unique *Vouliagmeni Lake*, and some of the best hotels in Attica. Athenians visit the coast and have lunch at a restaurant or a drink at a bar by the seaside.

Near the attractive suburbs of **Varkiza** are a multitude of small picturesque bays, ideal places to go for a swim.

You may reach the southern suburbs by bus using lines, among others, **No 155, 103, E2Θ**, and tram (lines **A1** and **A2** to Neo Faliro and Glyfada). Enjoy a unique walk along the coastal area!

MUSEUMS

THE NATIONAL ARCHAEOLOGICAL MUSEUM

The completely renovated National Archaeological Museum ranks among the leading archaeological museums in the world. Survey the numerous important exhibits and explore Greece's history. You will be impressed by the treasures of the museum and will want to come back for another visit. However, if you come just once, be sure to have enough time. We list some of the exhibits of the museum:

The statuette of Zeus.

The statuette of the Zeus Keravnovolos (casting lightning) from Dodoni. Notice the stance of the god as he prepares to cast lightning. It is the same as Poseidon of Artemision.

Demeter and Persephone.

This attractive, well-preserved relief from Eleusis was sculpted from around 440-430 BC. It depicts Demeter giving hay to the Triptolemos, the young king of Eleusis. To her right, her daughter Persephone gives her blessing. Notice that the Triptolemos and Demeter have different sizes. In that period artists made gods taller when they were depicted with mortals on a stele (dedicatory column) - a sign of respect of the gods.

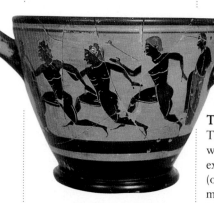

115. National Archaeological Museum: a Black Figure cup with a depiction of runners (circa 540 BC).

The Poseidon of Artemision.

Is it a statue of Poseidon or Zeus? Archaeologists have not come up with an answer. The bronze statue, a masterpiece of the sculpture of the classical period, is 2.09 metres high. It is one of the few preserved original bronze statues.

The lekythos of Myrrine.

The main exhibit in room 16, which is named after the exhibit. The particular lekythos (oil-flask), sculpted of white marble, was discovered in 1873. It is decorated with a sculpture representing Hermes driving with one hand a young woman, Myrrine. According to the epigram located on her head, the god's purpose was to bring the woman to Pluton (god of Hades). Three men, relatives of Myrrine observe the spectacle. (430-420 BC).

The stele of Hegeso. Don't fail to see the famous column of Hegeso (5th century BC). It was discovered in Kerameikos. There is replica of the column in Kerameikos. The sculpture depicts Hegeso seated, taking a jewel from a box. A female slave is holding the box It is thought that the colours used for the background of the sculpture and the jewel are blue and gold respectively. On the upper section of the column is carved the name "Hegeso Proxeno." Notice the artful depiction of her melancholy expression and the folds of her dress.

The "Jockeyboy" of Artemision.
The bronze statue of the 2nd century BC and a statue of Poseidon were discovered in the vicinity of Cape Artemision. The horseman and his horse may have been casted separately. Notice the excellent depiction of the extended muscles of the horse and the expression of agony on the horseman's face.

Marble votive relief. Demeter, Persephone and Asklepios.
Persephone stands to the left, holding two torches in her right hand. In front of her sits Demeter and to her right stands Asklepios. To the right are six suppliants who, according to the inscription, dedicated the sculpture to Asklepios and the two Eleusinian deities. Their names are carved on the pedestal encompassed by crowns made of olive branches.

The head of Hygeia.
Discovered in the temple of Alea Athena in Tegea the head of Hygeia was apparently part of a statue (350-340 BC). You will recognise the head of Hygeia (the goddess of health), which has been reproduced in photographs.

The Boy of Marathon.
The statue of a youth took was named after the bay of Marathon, where it was discovered in 1926. The inscription on the pedestal states that he is a wrestler. Excepting for the left hand, which is thought to be the produce of a posterior repair, the statue is thought to be a masterpiece. It is thought to be the work of Praxiteles, or one of his students (330BC).

116. National Archaeological Museum: the marble funerary column of a running soldier (Athens, circa 500 BC).
▼

81

117. National Archaeological Museum: "The Ephebe of Antikythera".

The Ephebe of Antikythera (ephebe: adolescent).

Archaeologists have varying opinions regarding the significance of the statue. The main subject holds a spherical object in his hand. Some archaeologists claim that the statue depicts the god Pan holding an apple, while others claim that it is the statue of Perseus holding the head of Andromedea (340BC). It was found in a shipwreck in the vicinity of Antikythera in 1900.

The golden mask of "Agamemnon."

Although it has been proven that it is not the mask of Agamemnon, it is a noteworthy exhibit, well worth seeing. Schlieman's theory was mistaken – today it is thought to be the mask of a dead king, who died three centuries before Agamemnon (16th century BC). You can see the mask and other objects (among others, jewels, golden works of art and swords), found in the royal graves of Mycenae, in the Gallery of Mycenaean Antiquities, facing the entrance.

The exhibition of Thera.

The main exhibits of the exhibition are the frescoes, which are a valuable source of information on life in the Aegean in the Bronze Age. They were discovered in the Cape of Thera (Santorini). They are the earliest examples of large-scale painting in Europe.

The fresco of spring: Depicts a rocky landscape with vivid red lilies and swallows, some flying in pairs some on their own.

The fresco of the fisherman: One of the best preserved frescoes, it depicts a nude fisherman holding two strings of fish.

The fresco of two children boxing: Two children boxing. The child standing to the left wears boxing gloves and earrings. Notice their almond-shaped eyes.

Epigraphical Museum.

A section of the Archaeological Museum, with a separate entrance. Displaying 14,000 epigraphs from Greece and Asia Minor, it is leading epigraphical museum.

THE GOULANDRIS MUSEUM OF CYCLADIC AND ANCIENT GREEK ART

The well-organised museum was founded with the purpose of housing the "Goulandris" private collection of Cycladic Art. It is one of the leading museums in Athens.

Exhibits. On the *1st floor* you will find various relics of Cycladic civilisation, while on the *2nd floor* are miniatures and other objects of the same period. On the *3rd floor* are temporary exhibitions of the museum while on the *4th floor* is the K. Politis collection of ancient Greek art. In 1992 a new wing was added to the Museum, at the **Stathatos Mansion**. In the new wing you can see the Academy of Athens collection of ancient Greek art. On the basement of the building at N. Douka you can buy replicas of museum exhibits.

THE NUMISMATIC MUSEUM

It is one of the five most important numismatic museums in the world. It displays more than 600,000 coins, "treasures" (closed coin collections), standard weights, metals and precious stones, from the ancient Greek period, the Roman period, Byzantium, the western Middle Ages, and modernity.

118. Numismatic Museum: Athenian four-drachma coin (440-430 BC).

83

THE ARCHAEOLOGICAL COLLECTIONS IN THE METRO

The biggest excavation ever in Greece was dug at the time of the construction of the metropolitan railway of Athens (1993-2000). Some of the approximately 50,000 finds that were uncovered in these excavations are exhibited in specially designed spaces in the metro stops **"Panepistimio," "Syntagma," Akropoli"** and **"Evangelismos"**.

◄

119. The entrance of Stathatos Mansion at Vassilisis Sophias

120. Historical and Ethnological Museum: the portrait of Lord Byron.

▼

THE HISTORICAL AND ETHNOLOGICAL MUSEUM

Located at Kolokotroni Square (●❖ *page 35*). The stately neoclassical building accommodating the Museum since 1961, was built from 1858-1871. The designs of the building produced by Fr. Boulanger, were modified by Greek architect P. Kalkos. Before 1935, the building was the seat of the Greek Parliament. The building is known as the Palaia Vouli (Old Parliament). The exhibits, displayed in 16 galleries, are from all periods of Greek history, from the 15th century AD.

THE BENAKI MUSEUM

One of the leading museums in Athens, the Benaki Museum is well worth a visit. It was founded by patrician Ant. Benakis (1873-1954) and inaugurated in 1931. It displays more than 45,000 exhibits of the collection of Ant. Benakis and other donors, organised in six collections:

Greece at the Benaki Museum. This section comprises of various categories with over 33,000 works, representative of Greek culture from antiquity to the creation of the modern Greek state and 1922 (the Asia Minor Disaster).

Hadjikyriakou-Gika Gallery. Granted by the famous Greek painter, the Hadjikyriakou-Gika Gallery is an annex of the museum. Housed in the building where the artist lived 40 years (at 3, Kriezotou Str), the gallery displays a representative example of his work.

Toys and Childhood. Included are 15,000 old toys and children's objects from Greece and the area of Greater Hellenism, from antiquity to 1970 – and Europe, America, Africa, and the countries of the East.

Coptic Art. A large collection of fabrics, metalwork and woodwork, representing the production of Egypt in the 5th and 6th centuries.

Chinese Art. Displays more than 1,300 exhibits (most of them were donated by G. Eumorfopoulos), representative of the Chinese civilisation from the 3rd Millennium BC to the 19th century (among others, vases, funeral statuettes, porcelain, miniatures and semi precious stones).

Islamic Art. This is one of the leading Islamic Art collections in the world. It displays more than 8,000 exhibits from Europe, the Middle East, North Africa, Persia and India, representative of the development of Islamic art from the early Islamic age to the 19th century.

Exhibitions. Sometimes the Benaki Museum holds important exhibitions in the central building or in other buildings.

Note: Some of the afore-mentioned collections may be transferred to other buildings belonging to the Benaki Museum. Please contact the Museum's information department before visiting the Museum.

THE BYZANTINE AND CHRISTIAN MUSEUM

The Museum houses one of the leading collections of Byzantine icons in the world. Its exhibits, representing 1500 years of Byzantine art and architecture, include ecclesiastical objects, mosaics, sculptures, frescoes and icons from Greece, the Balkans, Cyprus, Constantinople and Russia.

121. Benakis Museum: detail of the embroidery of a cushion (19th century).
◀

85

122. Byzantine and Christian Museum: icon of the 14th century, depicting the archangel Michael.

123. War Museum: a firearm of the first decades of the 20th century.

THE WAR MUSEUM

On display are weapons from the Stone Age and the Classical Age to the Second World War. Moreover, various kinds of aircraft, maps, flags, military uniforms and the models of warships and aircraft are displayed giving representative of Greek history.

THE NATIONAL GALLERY - ALEXANDROS SOUTZOS MUSEUM

It is the leading Gallery in Greece. The core of the collection comprises of 117 paintings, listed in 1878. Later the Gallery was enriched by private collections granted by Al. Soutzos, Eur. Koutlidis, and other Greek painters and collectors. A number of important works of art, such as the "Crucifixion" by Lorenzo Veneziano and a collection of engravings of the 16th and 20th centuries were acquired by the Gallery.

Well worth seeing are:

"The Kiss" by N. Lytras, "The Engagement," by N. Gyzis, "The Concert of Angels," by Dominicos Theotokopoulos and "The Greek Rider," by Delacroix.

124. The National Gallery is one of the vibrant cultural attractions of Athens.

NATIONAL MUSEUM OF MODERN ART

Accommodated in an old beer factory ("Fix"), the National Museum of Modern Art opened in 2000. It displays the works of Greek and foreign artists, and holds important temporary exhibitions.
The complete renovation of the building and the installation of its permanent collections will be completed in 2006.

THE FRISSIRAS MUSEUM

The only Museum of Contemporary European Painting in Greece, the Frissiras Museum is housed in two neoclassical buildings in Plaka. The collections include paintings, drawings, sculpture, and engravings of major European and Greek artists (among others, Hockney, Auerbach, Blake, Rustin, Pat Andrea, Dado, Rego, Arroyo, Adami, Diamantopoulou, Moralis, Mauroidis, Theofylaktopoulou, Botsoglou, Byzantiou).

THE MUSEUM OF GREEK FOLK ART

The remarkable collections of this museum are dated from 1650. The museum displays woven items, embroidery, uniforms, silver and puppet theatre. Moreover, the works of Theofilos Hadjimichael, woodcuts and sculpted stones are displayed.

THE MUSEUM OF THE CITY OF ATHENS

The museum is accommodated in a neoclassical building constructed in 1833 (*Vourou Mansion*, at Klafthmonos Square), which was used as King Otto's temporary palace from 1836-1842. You will find here paintings and engravings connected to the history of the Greek capital, mainly from the early 18th century to the 20th century. Moreover, furniture belonging to the first King of Greece, Otto is displayed.

▲
125. The inner yard and cafe of the Frissiras Museum.

THE MUSEUM OF GREEK TRADITIONAL MUSICAL INSTRUMENTS

Accommodated in an unadorned mansion built in 1842, at Aerides Square, the museum displays 1,200 folk musical instruments of the F. Anogeiannakis collection. Every showcase has audio. You can hear excerpts of songs played on the exhibited instruments. At the shop you will find CDs, selected books and copies of the musical instruments.

THE GENNADIUS LIBRARY COLLECTION

The collection includes valuable manuscripts and books, documents, periodicals, maps of the most important periods of Greek literature. Moreover, you will find here a Byzantine library, a reading room and an exhibition room. Well worth seeing is the collection of the personal objects of Lord Byron (golden clock, laurel wreath, seals, etc).

THE FOUNDATION OF THE HELLENIC WORLD

The Foundation of the Hellenic World was established in 1993, with a view to preserve, and inform the public on Greek history and culture using modern technological means. The Cultural Centre "The Greek World" was established. The Foundation, among others, presents Greek history on the Internet from the Stone Age, digitally reproducing ancient monuments and spaces, projecting historical and cultural documentaries, organising exhibitions and educational programmes and staging cultural tours by means of the Virtual Reality systems "Ark" and "Magic Screen".

126. The Vorres Museum.

127. The Goulandris Museum of Natural History: an aerial photograph of the "Gaia" centre.

THE VORRES MUSEUM

Six thousand exhibits, representing 40 centuries of Greek history, are displayed in the Museum. The area of the Museum is 4,500 square metres. It is divided in two sections.

In the **first section** you will find a collection of modern Greek art comprising of paintings and sculptures of the late 20th century.

The **second section** is housed in a complex of two traditional village houses and a building, which was formerly used as a winepress. You will find here household objects, such as carpets, furniture, millstones, and ceramic art works from various areas of Greece. Moreover, in the section are exhibited oil paintings and engravings connected to historical events, and certain archaeological finds.

THE GOULANDRIS NATURAL HISTORY MUSEUM ("GAIA" CENTRE)

In this important Museum you can learn about the interdependence of living organisms. The museum displays rich collections of insects, mammals, serpents, birds, and shells, and rocks and fossils from Greece. Moreover, it organises seminars and lectures and holds temporary exhibitions connected to environmental issues relating to Greece and the world.

"Gaia" Centre. Recently, the Museum opened the Centre of Environmental Research and Education "Gaia." Visitors are offered a glimpse of the workings of nature. Educational programmes are also held at the building. The area of the building is 12,500 square metres and also has permanent exhibition areas (energy, transport, natural recources, water, food).

DAY TRIPS IN ATTICA

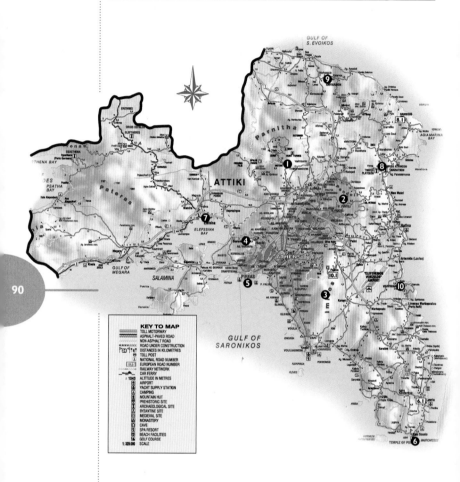

Greater Attica, an area of natural beauty, has been since antiquity the most important cultural centre of Greece. With important historical and archaeological sites, unique Byzantine monuments, mountains, fertile plains and clean beaches – all easily accessible from Athens – Attica is an attractive destination for day trips, offering an escape from the busy streets of Athens.

❶ MOUNT PARNITHA

If you like nature, hiking in the mountains, collecting herbs, or gambling, Mount Parnitha is the place for you. Mount Parnitha (1,400 metres), the most beautiful mountain of Greece, is located 30 kilometres northwest of Athens. Mount Parnitha National Park has an area of more than 300 square kilometres, and more than 800 kinds of herbs and plants, (including 17 % of the flora of Greece). Walk on one of hundreds of footpaths and explore dozens of small caves.

Ancient Greeks believed that the goat-footed god Pan often came to play music and dance in the forest of Parnitha. Parnitha was first inhabited in the Mycenaean Age. It was a key location for the defence of Attica. It was the most fortified mountain of ancient Greece.

Visit the luxury hotel "Mont Parnes" and try your luck at the Casino. If you like walking you can visit the mountain huts of *Bafi* and *Flambouri*.

The "Mont Parnes" Casino.
The casino is open daily except Wednesdays. Visitors should wear evening dress and carry a valid passport. Tel. 210 24 21 234.

 GETTING THERE:

If you use your own car, follow the National Road towards Lamia and take a left turn at the Parnitha exit. The road leading to the top follows a picturesque route, with many turns. If you do not want to take your car to the top, park at the foot of the mountain and take the funicular (tel. 210 24 21 234). **Bus number 714** from Vathi Square (Athens) reaches the top of the mountain in about two hours.

128. Climbing the craggy rocks of Parnitha.

❷ MOUNT PENTELI

Penteli is a densely vegetated mountain with springs and attractive locations. You have a spectacular view of the city and the Euboean Gulf from the top. Penteli is known as a source of marble. Pentelic Marble was the main material used for the construction of all attic architectural and sculptural marvels of the classical period. The unique white colour of Pentelic marble was well known in antiquity. Pentelic marble was an important export product of ancient Athens. Later it was used in the construction of the Panathenaikon (Kallimarmaron) Stadium, which was the location of the 1st modern Olympics (1896), revived by the French baron Pierre de Coubertin.

☞ THE SIGHTS:

The Penteli Monastery.
The wealthiest and biggest monastery in Greece, Penteli Monastery was founded in 1578 by Archbishop Timotheos. It is dedicated to the Assumption of the Virgin Mary. A number of buildings were added to the original structure. Sections of the original building were later reconstructed. Recently a multitude of new buildings were added for the monks staying at the monastery. Visitors may see the original hospital, fountain and some of the cells.

 GETTING THERE:

Take **bus number A6** or **E6** from Athens (Vassilisis Irakleiou Str, in the vicinity of the Archaeological Museum) to Halandri Square, and change to **bus number 423 or 426**.

❸ MOUNT HYMETTOS

Mount Hymettos is located south of the Athens basin. It is linked to the history of Athens. Sanctuaries have been built here since antiquity (among others, the sanctuaries of Zeus and Pan). Moreover, in the western side were marble mines. Marble was used for the construction of monuments in the Hellenistic and roman periods. Hymettos has abundant vegetation and a large variety of fauna and flora. In the past few decades, the state has introduced special measures to protect the important ecology of Mount Hymettos. Hymettos is the most popular destination in the vicinity of Athens, combining natural beauty with a multitude of archaeological finds and important Byzantine monasteries.

☞ THE SIGHTS:

The Ayios Ioannis Kynigos Monastery.
Located at the northern peak of Hymettos, with a view of Athens and the Mesoghia Plain, the monastery was possibly built in the 12th century. Only the central church (built of plinth), which has been modified, and the main entrance (13th century), remains of the old monastery. The monastery accommodates a women's commune. Access to the monastery from *Ayia Paraskevi* (open 8:00-12:00 pm and 16:00-19:00).

The Ayiou Ioanni Theologou Monastery.
The monastery is located in the vicinity of the perimeter of the *Papagou* suburb. You can get there via Anastaseos Str. The monastery was built on the site of an ancient building (you will find here, among others, ancient capital, pedestals). The main cruciform church, is dated to the late Byzantine period (13th- 15th century). The monastery accommodates a women's commune. It is closed at mid-day (12:00-16:00).

The Asteriou Monastery.
Located north of Aghios Ioannis Theologos, on a wooded slope, Asteriou Monastery is thought to have been founded in the 5th century. The building complex, which has been preserved, includes a four-side fort-style court, two wings with buildings and a main church, built in cruciform style, with interesting frescoes of the 16th century.

A domed cistern with a fountain from the period of Turkish occupation is preserved. The monastery has been designated a historical monument (open 08:00-15:00).

The Kaisariani Monastery.
Built in the 2nd century AD, the monastery is located in an idyllic location on the slopes of Mount Hymettos. According to Greek mythology, the god Hephaistos often came here. The riverbed of the river Ilissos, the sacred river of Aphrodite, is located on a hill above the monastery. The monastery was built on the ruins of a roman and late ancient Greek temple. Four columns of the ancient temple now support the dome of the church. In the late 12th century and early 13th century the monastery prospered and became an influential cultural and spiritual centre. The church of the monastery, dedicated to the Presentation of the Virgin

93

▲
129. Kaisariani Monastery.

130. The slopes of Hymettos. ▼

Mary, is built in the Hellenic cruciform style, and decorated with frescoes of the 16th century. On the western wall of the yard you will find a spring. The water gushes from the mouth of a marble goat. Formerly it was thought that the water cured infertility. It is thought that they have "magic" qualities. There is a spring at the stoup, a sanctuary on the northwest wall of the yard. Kaisariani Monastery is an excellent starting point for a hiking trip.

Ayios Ioannis Kareas Monastery.

The monastery, founded in 1550, is located a few hundred metres from the *Kareas* area. The main church, a two-storey wing of cells and a small one-floor building on the northern side is all that remains of the old complex. After the 1970's major reconstruction work was done on the old monastery and a new two-floor wing of cells was built. It is a women's monastery (opening hours 08:00-12:00 and 16:00-20:00).

Panos Cave (Nymfolyptou).

Located in the southeastern area of the mountain (3 kilometres north of the suburb of *Vari*). It was dedicated to Pan. The deity was worshiped there from 600 BC to 150 AC. Worth seeing are the unique sculptures and epigrams preserved on engravings in the rocks. The most important is an epigram by the sculptor Archedimos. Archaeologists researching the multiple finds (among others, clay oil lamps, stone offerings) deduced that the cave was used as a place of worship also in the Christian period.

The Botanical Garden.

Some 5 kilometres from the centre of Athens, you can enjoy a walk in an area with 3 million pine trees, cypress trees, fir trees, poplar trees, plane trees, and oak trees. Moreover, in the Botanical Garden are thousands of birds and wild flora. It is the ideal scene for a long walk and a picnic. You will find picnic tables and benches, after about 20 minutes of walking from Kaisariani Monastery.

❹ THE DAPHNI MONASTERY

Well worth your visit is the Daphni Monastery (11 kilometres from Athens, near the *Haidari* suburb, the Athens – Corinth National Road), which is linked to ancient mythology, the classical period, and Byzantine history. The Monastery is thought to be the most important Byzantine monument in the Athens area, while the mosaics are thought to be masterpieces of the golden age of Byzantine art.

Built on hallowed ground.

In the 2nd century AD, the geographer Pausanias referred to the Temple of Daphnaio or Daphnaeos Apollo, located in a sacred laurel thicket, by the Iera Odos (Iera Odos in Greek means Sacred Road), leading from Athens to Eleusis. The Goths destroyed the temple in 395 AD. Later, the Byzantine emperors banned idolatry. The Christians acquired the location and built a church, using the materials of the old temple. They selected this location because it was on the road to Eleusis, where the idolaters held the Eleusinian Mysteries. In 1100 AD a new octagonal church was built. The monastery was modified several times before the 19th century. In the Greek Revolution it was refuge of Greek freedom fighters.

The myths.

According to mythology, the location was named after the ancient temple and the laurel thicket. According to another myth, Daphni was named after Queen Daphne, whose boat was shipwrecked near the port of Eleusis. Queen Daphne was saved, and as an expression of gratitude to the god Apollo, she built the temple. The temple was later destroyed by the Goths. However, according to another myth, the place was named after the nymph Daphne, who escaped to the location from the god Apollo and was metamorphosed into a laurel tree.

☞ THE SIGHTS:

The mosaics. Daphni is famous for its unique and beautiful mosaics, created in the 11 century AD. You will see them on the walls, the dome, the arms of the cross the roof and the altar. Seventy-six of the subjects of the mosaics refer to the life of Christ and the Virgin Mary. Moreover, you can see

131. Detail of the unique mosaics of the Daphni Monastery.
▼

95

mosaics depicting saints and prophets.

Christ Pantokrator.
The central figure on the dome is the Pantokrator, encompassed by a circle symbolising the sky, while the golden font symbolises Paradise. Pantokrator's face is austere. He looks at the people on earth and judges their actions. He is surrounded by the prophets of the Old Testament.

The Assumption of the Virgin.
The mosaic is half destroyed. It is located on the western wall of the Church. Notice the angel descending from the sky to receive the soul of the Virgin. He is thoughtful. His hands are graciously covered by fabric.

❺ PIRAEUS

Most people have heard at least once the song "Ta Paidia tou Pirea," composed by M. Hadjidakis, with Melina Mercouri singing in the film "Never on Sunday." However, many people don't know the place, which the film and the movie made famous – the city and port of Piraeus.

The history of Piraeus.
Piraeus is encompassed almost on all sides by sea. The pace of life of Piraeus is linked to the sea. In antiquity it was an island. Travellers were ferried across to the mainland (in ancient Greek the word for ferried is

 GETTING THERE:

Bus number 812 to Haidari departs from Koumoundou-rou (Eleftherias) Square.

diepairounto). That perhaps explains the origin of its name.

The architect Ippodamos designed the urban planning of Piraeus in the mid 5th century BC. Ippodamos's plans were used as the guidelines for the reconstruction of the city in 1834. Themistocles was the first person to realise the importance of the role the city could play for Athens. He made Piraeus Athens's leading port, relegating the Bay of Faliron, which the Athenians used before the 5th century BC. Seeking to develop a fortified port for the city of Athens, from 493 to 479 BC he built the wall of Piraeus. Later Pericles completed the fortification, building the Long Walls, which protected both sides of the road from Piraeus to Athens. In the Middle Ages, Piraeus was named Porto Leone, after a giant stone lion, guarding the entrance of the harbour. Today it is the main port of Athens, the biggest port in Greece, one of the leading ports in the Mediterranean, an important centre of the merchant marine, industry and transportation. The centres of Piraeus are its three ports: the central port, the Zea marina, and Mikrolimano.

97

132. *The Zea harbour (or Pasalimani) is one of the central locations of the city of Piraeus.*

☞ THE SIGHTS:

The Central port. The ancient name of the central port was Kantharos. At present it is the centre of the city. You will find here ships to all the islands of the Aegean (excepting for the Sporades) and Crete. Walk around and look at the passenger and freight ships, and the arrivals and departures of merchandise and people from all the world. In the Freatyda area parts of the **Wall of Piraeus** (the coastal section) are preserved.

The Zea marina (Pasalimani). In this marina, some of the most impressive yachts and cruise ships anchor. At the seafront are restaurants, tavernas, bars and shops, catering to the needs of passengers. You will find Flying Dolphins (hovercrafts) serving lines to the Argosaronikos

Gulf. Adjacent to the Archaeological Museum is the **Ancient Theatre of Zea** (4th – 3rd century BC).

Mikrolimano. The port was protected by the goddess Mounihia Artemis. At present it is a popular location, attracting people from all over Attica. It is a beautiful little harbour with fishing boats, small boats and luxury yachts. If you like fish and seafood have lunch or dinner at one of its famous tavernas.

Kastella. An elegant and popular neighbourhood of Piraeus, built on a hill also known as Profitis Ilias. Walk to the top of the hill, and admire the alleys with picturesque houses. The view of the main port, Zea and Mikrolimano is unique. In the area is the open-air **theatre "Veakeio,"** which hosts important cultural events in summer.

The Municipal Theatre. It dominates one of the central squares (Korai Square). It was built in the 1880's in the neoclassical style by architect I. Lazarimos. It is one of the most frequented places, a meeting place of residents of Piraeus.

133. Piraeus: Municipal Theatre.

98

134: The renovated Piraeus metro station.

The I.S.A.P. station (metro stop "Piraeus"). The stately eclectic building with the arched dome (1929), replicates the relevant European stations of the period. Recently the interior was completely renovated. One the walls are displayed the works of the students of the School of Fine Arts.

Piraeus's "Monastiraki." A market similar to the corresponding market in Athens (Monastiraki), open every Sunday at Dragatsaniou Str. and Mavromihali Str. You can find good bargains.

The Archaeological Museum. It displays mostly sculptures found in Piraeus at the coast of Attica. The exhibits relate the history, and the rise and fall of the ancient city.

Notice the five bronze statue discovered in Piraeus in 1959. Archaic Kouros-Apollo, two statues of Artemis, Athena of Piraeus, and an ancient tragedy mask (4th century BC).

The Maritime Museum. The Maritime Museum is located at *Akti Moutsopoulou.* Its exhibits cover about 3,000 years of Greek nautical history.

99

 GETTING THERE:

You can take the metro and get off at the stop "Piraeus." There are bus lines from Athens to Akti Xaveriou in Piraeus. One line has its terminus at Syntagma Square **(number 40)** and another line has its terminus at Athenas Str. in the Omonia Square area **(number 49)**.

135: The ruins of the temple of Poseidon.

❻ SOUNION

The sanctuary of Sounion (the famous temple of Poseidon is here) is the most important sanctuary of Attica. Situated at a unique site (cape Sounio) the sanctuary is one of the major sights of Greece. It is one hour's drive from the centre of Athens. The route to Sounion follows the coastline of the Saronic Gulf. Look out of the window of your car or bus and you will enjoy the sparkling blue sea. If you travel by car, you can stop and go for a swim in a organised beach or one of the beautiful little bays located at many places on your way. You will also find here a multitude of cafes, tavernas serving fresh fish and ouzo restaurants.

☞ T H E   S I G H T S :

The Temple of Poseidon.

At this site the ancient Greeks worshipped the god of the sea, Poseidon. Preserved are 15 Doric style columns (originally there were 34). The temple was built in the Golden Age of Perikles on the ruins of another temple. We do not know who the architect is. However, it is thought that it is the architect who designed the Theseion. Following an examination of the finds unearthed in the area archaeologists have deduced that Poseidon was worshipped here before the 5th century BC.

The temple of goddess Athena.
Worth your visit is the temple of Athena Sounias, located at a distance of 400

metres from the temple of Poseidon. You will find here the substructures of two temples: a large temple built at around 470 BC or during the Peloponnesean War (431-404), and a small temple. Archaeologists have diverging opinions regarding the small temple: some believe it is the ruin of an old temple dedicated to Athena, and built in the period 600-550 BC, other believe the temple was dedicated to Artemis.

6.1 LAVRION

Located approximately 9 kilometres northeast of Sounio is Lavrion, a small picturesque town with a multitude of neoclassical houses and mansions, which was famous in antiquity for its mines. The mines of Lavrion closed in the 1970's. At the perimeter of the city is the *Technological Cultural Part* of Lavrion, including industrial units of the period 1875-1940. Worth a visit is the *Mineralogical Museum* (Andr. Kordelas Avenue). At the seafront are a multitude of traditional cafes and fish tavernas, with delicious snacks. Some 4 kilometres north of Lavrion is the *archaeological site of Thorikos*. In the area encompassed by Lavrion and Sounion is the *Sounion National Park*, with natural and cultural attractions.

⇨ **GETTING THERE:**

Two bus lines link Sounio to Athens: one route via, the coastal road of Varkiza and Legrena, and another via the inland of Attica, namely Agia Paraskevi, Koropi and Lavrio. The terminus of both bus lines is located at Mavromataion Str. in the vicinity of Pedion tou Areos in Athens (tel. 210 82 30 179). Moreover, travel agents organise day trips to the temple of Poseidon.

101

136: Blue sky and blue sea are joined at Cape Sounion.

137. View of the sanctuary of Eleusis.

❼ ELEUSIS (or ELEUSINA)

Eleusina is an industrial town located 23 kilometres west of Athens. Founded in the 2nd millennium BC, the sanctuary became pan-Hellenic in the 8th century BC. Uninitiated visitors will not appreciate its glorious past, the history and the mythology regarding the local gods, the deities and the worship thereof.

Demeter and Persephone.

The citizens of Eleusina worshipped Demeter, the goddess of nature, spring and agriculture. The myth of Demeter and her daughter Persephone is, like most myths, allegorical. It refers to the rebirth of plant life, following its "death" in winter, and the eternal longing for immortality. According to a hymn of the 7th century BC, one day the earth opened up in two, Plouton, the god of the underworld appeared, and seized the young Persephone. He took her to his kingdom and made her his wife. Her mother looked for her in despair. She looked for her nine days and nights, without success. She arrived despairing at the doorstep of the palace of Keleos, king of Elefsina. She became the nurse of his son, not revealing that she is a deity. When her real identity was revealed, she requested that a temple be built in her honour. She remained in the temple, devastated by the loss of her daughter. The following year, not a seed grew on the world. Zeus was worried. He sent Hermes to appeal to Plouton. A compromise was reached:

Persephone would remain in the kingdom of Pluto 1/3 of the year, and the remaining time she could stay with her mother. Overjoyed, Demeter allowed the plants and flowers to grow, and the earth became fruitful.

The Mysteries of Eleusina.

The Eleusinian Mysteries were named mysteries because the most important part of the event, involved intense mysticism. We don't know much about the worship of Demeter by thousands of people over 15 centuries. The Great Eleusinian Mysteries had their starting point in Eleusina. The remarkable procession moved on to Athens, headed by the priestess and the sacred symbols of the worship of Demeter. The Mysteries were concluded with ceremonies in honour of the dead. After the ceremony, Athenians returned to Athens. The Eleusinian Mysteries were abolished in the 4th century BC by the Byzantine emperor Theodosios.

☞ THE SIGHTS:

The Archaeological site.

During your visit, bear in mind that the greater part of the area was avaton – a place inaccessible to the uninitiated - many centuries. Worth seeing are the remains of the *Telesterion* (ceremonial chamber), also known as the Iero ton Mystirion, located in the centre of the area, the *Ieri Avli*, the *Great and Small Propylaea*, and *Ploutoneio*.

The Archaeological Museum.

Displayed at the Museum of Eleusina are the finds of the digs of the sanctuary and the western cemetery. Worth seeing is the *Protoattic Amphora of Eleusina* (650 BC). The neck of the amphora is decorated by a depiction of the blinding of the Cyclops Polyfemos by Ulysses. On the main body of the amphora, Perseus beheads Medusa. Also worth seeing is the *Kore* from the pediment of the *Ieri Oikia* (Ieri Oikia in Greek means Sacred House) (490-480 BC). It is the statue of a running maiden, her head turned to the left.

103

 GETTING THERE:

If you travel by car, take the Athens-Corinth National Road. The bus to Corinth (**number A16** and **B16**) has its terminus at Koumoundourou Square in Athens.

138. The Marathon Archaeological Museum: clay vase of the Neolithic period from the Cave of Pan (Oini).
▼

❽ MARATHON

Well worth your visit is Marathon, with an archaeological area and museum. Marathon is one of the most beautiful locations in Attica. The way to Marathon is beautiful. On your way you will pass by fields, vineyards, olive groves, wild vegetation, giving the area its natural beauty. You will find here a multitude of beaches where you can swim and sunbathe. The most famous beach is *Schinias* (an exceptionally beautiful location), which has a pine forest bordering on the sandy shore. You can combine a visit to Marathon with a visit the archaeological area of Ramnounda. (12 kilometres from Marathon).

The battle of Marathon.

The main source of information regarding the battle of Marathon is the ancient historian Herodotus. According to Herodotus, the Persian fleet disembarked 100,000 troops in Marathon in 490 BC. Facing this immense army were just 11,000 Greek troops (10,000 were from Athens and 1,000 from Plataiai). The Greeks, thanks to the military genius of Miltiades, won the battle. Following the victory, Pheidippides, an Athenian soldier, was sent to bring the good news to the city. He ran all the way from the field of battle to the Athenian Agora. He said one word: Nenikikamen (we have won), collapsed and passed away. In memory of the event, the modern Marathon covers the distance Pheidippides ran, and is symbolised in the closing ceremony of the Olympic Games.

☞ T H E   S I G H T S :

The Monument (Tomb) of Marathon.
Adjacent to the field of battle, at a distance of one kilometre from Marathon, you will find a unique monument (Tomb) of the 192 Athenian soldiers who died in the battle. On the other side of the road, at a distance of 5 kilometres, is the grave of the Plataians.

The Archaeological Museum of Marathon.
The museum is small. It houses exhibits from nearby towns, as well as other periods and

locations. Important finds of the Neolithic Age, such as the finds discovered at the cave of Pan in Oenoe, and a collection of columns, thought to have been built in the 2nd century BC, are also on display.

8.1 ➤ RAMNOUS (KATO SOULI)

The name of the area is derived from the word 'ramnos,' the name of a variety of bush covering the area. In antiquity, Ramnous was known for its port and fort. In the archaeological area are the ruins of two temples. The Great temple was dedicated to Nemesis, the goddess of Divine Justice (it was the most important sanctuary of the goddess in ancient Greece). The small temple was dedicated to Themis, the goddess of Justice. Both temples were built in the 5th century BC. The remains of a fort, theatre, funerary monuments, among others, are preserved. The view of Euboea and the Euboean Gulf from the large pine tree - located in the vicinity of the temple - is unique.

GETTING THERE:

You can take the bus to Paralia Marathona, from Mavromataion Str. (Aigyptou Square) near Paidio tou Areos.
Tel. 210 82 10 872.

❾ AMPHIAREION

Amphiaraos is one of the least well-known deities of ancient mythology. Nevertheless, he was popular, and twelve temples and sanctuaries are known to have been dedicated to him. His popularity was due to his magical and healing qualities. According to myth, he was not born, but emerged from a spring, located near his temple, in the vicinity of Oropos. He participated in the expedition of the Argonauts, and later in the siege of Thebes by the Argeans. In the latter Zeus intervened, saving Amphiaraos's life. The most important temple dedicated to Amphiaraos if Amphiareion, located in a gorge on the border of Attica and Boeotia. An *ancient theatre* with a capacity of 3,000 dominates the area. Notice the five white marble seats around the scene, with sculpted decoration and epigraphs. The temple is located in the vicinity of a spring, mentioned in the myth of Amphiaraos. It was built in the

105

139. Theatre at Amphiareion archaeological site.

Doric style in the 4th century BC. Most of the ruins in the area were dated to 6th century BC.

> ➡️ **GETTING THERE:**
>
> Amphiareion is located 48 kilometres from Athens. If you have a car, take the Athens-Lamia National road, and take a turn left on the road to Oropos. Two bus lines link Athens to Oropos, both with a stop in the vicinity of the Aphmiareion archaeological area. Walk another 3 kilometres from the bus stop to the archaeological site. Two alternative bus lines link Athens to Ayioi Apostoloi (get off at Oropos, at a distance of 3.3 kilometres from the archaeological site), and Oropos. You can get off the bus at the Marcopoulo cemetery, at a distance of 3 kilometres from the location. You will find the terminus of the buses at Mavromataion Str. in Athens (Aigyptou Square) tel 210 82 30 179.

⑩ VRAVRON

Vravrona, with an interesting archaeological site, is well worth a visit. On your way to Vravrona, you will travel through one of the most beautiful areas of Attica, with green fields, vineyards, olive trees, gentle mountainsides, and the coast of the blue Euboean Gulf. In summer, if you don't like the heat, you can take a dip in the sea. Be sure to follow the signposts leading to Marko-poulo and Limani Mesogheas, then take a turn left at the sign for Vravrona. A few kilometres inland is the archaeological site and the museum on your left.

Artemis Vravronia. Vravron was dedicated to Artemis, the goddess protector of hunters, animals and the safe birth of humans. Enraged by the murder of two small female bears, Artemis caused an epidemic in Athens. She requested that an oracle tell the Athenians that all girls aged 5 to 10 living in Attica were obliged to worship her. The Athenians obeyed the command of the goddess and brought their little girls to the temple, where they spend their childhood years serving her and participating in the festivals organised there. The girls who went to the temple, were called arktoi (bears). The festivals in honour of the goddess were called Vravronia. Musical performances, athletic compe-titions and poetry readings were held at the festivals.

☞ T H E   S I G H T S :

Archaeological site. You will notice the coexistence of the ruins of the ancient Greek temple of Artemis and a Christian church of the 15th century AD, dedicated to Ayios Georgios. Unfortunately only the sanctuary of the ancient temple is preserved. Archaeologists have not determined the shape of the original temple. Walk over a bridge, built in the classical period, which leads, to the temple, and visit the partially renovated colonnade.

The Museum. Small and interesting, the museum houses exhibits from the Vravron area and Anavyssos, Perati and other areas of Attica.

10.1 ➤ PAIANIA CAVE (KOUTOUKI)

With a large variety of rocks and the multiformity of the stalagmites and stalagmites, Koutouki Cave ranks among of the most interesting caves n Greece. Located on the eastern slope of Mount Hymettos, at an altitude of 540 metres, 4 kilometres from *Paiania* in the Mesoghia area, it has a total area of 3,800 square metres.

⇨ **GETTING THERE:**

Vravron is located 38 kilometres from Athens. If you have a car, take Mesogheion Avenue, and following the suburb of Agia Paraskevi, take a turn right on the road to Markopoulo-Porto Rafti. A bus line links the area to Athens. It departs every hour from Mavroma-taeon Str. (Pedion tou Areos – tel. 210 82 30 179).

107

▲
*140. Vravrona:
at Arkton
Collonade
resided young
girls dedicated
to the goddess
Artemis.*

THE SARONIC ISLANDS

Boats, ferries and flying dolphins depart daily from the port of Piraeus for the islands of the Saronic Gulf, *Salamina, Aegina, Angistri, Hydra, Poros* and *Spetses*. Moreover, tourist offices organise daily cruises to these islands.

SHOPPING IN ATHENS

141. At "Giousouroum, one of the most charming neighbourhoods of Athens, you can find a multitude of old objects.

▶

108

142. Modern shopping centers like this are found in most areas of Athens and its suburbs.

You will be surprised at the bargains you will find in Athens. Golden and silver jewellery are popular, given the international renown of Greek designers. A multitude of jewellers shops most of them located in the Syntagma Square and Kolonaki areas, have a wide selection of reproductions of ancient Greek jewels and traditional and modern designs. Most of them are hand made by local craftsmen. Moreover, at a multitude of Greek shops you can find silver and turquoise filigrans, most of them made in the city of Ioannina, in Epirus, with attractive traditional motifs.

Worth a visit is the *Ilias Lalaounis Jewellery Museum*. The Museum houses more than 3,000 designs of jewels.

Some 45 collections representing the history of Greek jewellery inspired by the art and architecture of eleven civilisations, nature, technology and biology.

You may be interested in the famous furs of Kastoria, the product of an craft that was perfected over the centuries. In the Syntagma Square area is a multitude of fur shops offering a wide range of coats, jackets and fur hats, with classic and modern designs. You may also find bargain souvenirs, hand made goods and bronze vases. Athens has been famous for its copper utensils, clay and ceramic goods since the Archaic Age. The ideal place to find unique items of Greek ceramic art and pottery is the suburb of Maroussi, where most

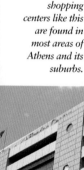

designers and ceramicists have shops offering hand made goods.

You may also find bargain quality woven wool and cotton jumpers with unique designs and leather goods and shoes made by Greek designers.

You will find these items at Ermou Str. and Kolonaki Square. You will also find an abundance of antiques in various shops in Kolonaki, Syntagma and Monastiraki. You may find various kinds of antiques, such as furniture, hand painted wooden trunks, attractive miniatures, and small decorative items.

The National Council of Social Care.

Here you will find valuable hand made heavy carpets and rugs made on wooden looms, and a wide range of embroidery, embroidered tapestries, hand made cushions and bags, decorative wall embroideries and uniquely charming, authentic designs of Greek popular art.

14, Filellinon Str.
Tel. 210 3250240-1, 197.

The Hellenic Organisation of Small Medium Sized Enterprises and Handicrafts (EOMMEX).

You will find here attractive, quality, and hand made carpets. EOMMEX has established workshops in the country teaching the art of traditional carpet making. You will be impressed by the superb designs, the lively colours and quality of the materials used for EOMMEX carpets. In the shop at Mitropoleos Str you will find a large variety of designs and sizes. You are sure to find a good bargain.

9, Metropoleos Str.
Tel. 210 3230408.

109

◄

143. Ermou Street is a very busy street most of the year. It is the location of a multitude of well-known shops.

NIGHT LIFE

144. The bouzouki, an integral part of Greek popular music.

145. A classical music concert at the Odeion of Herodes Atticus (with a capacity of 4,500), below the floodlit Acropolis.

Athens never sleeps. Some people say that Athens is more vibrant at night. Ancient and modern Athens offers more opportunity for nightlife than any other city. You have a lot of options: ancient Greek drama in a theatre dated to the period the play was written, world famous orchestras playing music ranging from Beethoven and jazz in one of the most modern concert halls of Europe, unique musical stages and clubs offering variety and creativity.

The capital of Athens offers nightlife fans special nights out. Whatever you choose to do, you will discover that Athens nightlife offers variety and unique choice, making it possible to enjoy throughout the night. The only problem is that the following day you have to see the sights… You can start your evening out at one of the select restaurants or one of the distinctive Greek tavernas located in every neighbourhood of the city. The atmosphere in Greek restaurants is relaxed and friendly and the food is excellent. You may go to a taverna with live bouzouki music, or one of hundreds of popular, modern bars, clubs, disco-bars and bars with live music, featuring all varieties of music. You can find bars in all central areas, and all the suburbs, (among others, Kifissia, Faliro, Vouliagmeni, Voula, Varkiza).

A night out at place with live bouzouki music is an unforgettable experience. During your visit, you should go to a bouzouki joint, listen to authentic Greek music, sing and dance with the patrons in the joint.

GREEK CUISINE AND WINE

Greek cuisine has a unique flavour. During your stay in Greece you will be pleasantly surprised by culinary specialities. "Mousaka," "souvlaki," "Greek salad," is all most people know of Greek cuisine. However, you will discover that Greek cuisine comprises of a large variety of dishes fully meeting the culinary appetites of meat-eaters and vegetarians.

This is not surprising considering that Greece is the country where symposiums originated and the homeland of the Epikureian philosophers. Archestratos wrote the first cookbooks in history in 330 BC reminding readers that cuisine is a mark of civilisation. Greece has a gastronomic tradition of 4,000 years. However, like most national cuisines, Greek cuisine was influenced by neighbouring countries, from the East and the West.

TRADITIONAL GREEK CUISINE

Greek cuisine is unique because it combines the following features: unique ingredients, Greek dietary habits, the custom of making a meal a social event, and the pleasant atmosphere of Greece.

The basic ingredients.
Greek cuisine has four secrets. Good fresh ingredients, the proper use of aromatic herbs and spices, the famous Greek olive oil and simplicity. Greek olive oil deserves a special mention. It accompanies nearly all Greek dishes. It is usually used in large measures. Greece has high quality, healthy olive oil. The artificial cultivation of vegetables is not widespread in Greece because of the mildness of the climate. Most vegetables are cultivated in a natural way, preserving their aroma and taste. You will be delighted by the taste of Greek tomatoes, cabbage, carrots, onions, parsley, and garlic, not to mention fresh Greek fruit, such as, among others, grapes, apricots, peaches, cherries, melons, and water-melons. The aromatic herbs, which most Greeks pick in the mountains or the country, have a unique flavour, aroma and therapeutic qualities. You will be delighted by the intoxicating aroma of oregano, thyme, mint, and rosemary, in a large variety of dishes. Don't forget to try Greek cheeses, in

The general atmosphere.
Try a glass of ouzo or wine with fried octopus or any other Greek dish, sitting in the shade of a tree in a small taverna by the seafront, on an Aegean island. Try to repeat the experience in your home country, preparing the same dish, and helping yourself to the same drink. You may try it anywhere, but you will soon realise that the flavour is not the same. Don't try again. Your palate has not changed, nor is there something lacking in your cooking skills. The Greek food experience, in particular the combination of what you eat and where you eat it, are unique, and cannot be exported or imitated. It is simply something you can find, taste and enjoy only in Greece.

particular, feta. Meat has unique flavour because sheep and goats graze on open fields, and grazing meadows are verdant. Mediterranean seafood tastes much better than ocean seafood. The Aegean Sea and Ionian Sea, are clean seas, abundant in fish. Fresh fish fried on charcoal is a speciality.

The Greek attitude.
Greeks religiously preserved the custom of gathering around the table to enjoy a meal or various appetisers, (mezedes), with ouzo. Having a meal with friends at home or at a restaurant or taverna is a deeply rooted social habit. The Greek word symposium, recalling the ancient origins of Greece, translated word for word means "drinking with company." The atmosphere in typical Greek restaurants and tavernas is casual, relaxed and informal. Food is prepared according to fundamental rules. Good amateur cooks enjoy great respect in their social circle, while a good housewife in Greece means a good cook. A good cook sometimes dedicates days to the preparation of a meal for his friends.

112

▲
146. The enjoyment of a good meal with friends is a distinctive Greek custom.

GREEK WINE

Greece, the country of Dionysos, the god of wine, is the home of the first Vins de Qualite Produit Region (VQPRD) wines in history. The wines in question were from the islands of Hios and Thasos, famous in antiquity. For a variety of historical and social reasons, and due to natural disasters, the art of wine-making declined from the mid-19th century to the early 1960's. Then the traditional customs of wine-making revived. Today you can find a multitude of excellent Greek wines from every region of the country. When you taste Greek wine, bear in mind that it is the produce of excellent harvest, made from varieties of grape unknown to Western lovers of wine.
Greek wines are categorised as follows:

1) Controlled Appellation of Origin.

2) Superior Quality Appellation of Origin

3) Local wine.

4) Table wine.

Controlled appellation of origin

Listed in the category are only sweet wines, such as the Mavrodaphne of Cephalonia and Patra, the Moshato of Patras, Limnos, Cephalonia and Rodos, and the Sweet wine of Samos.

Listed in the category of **superior quality appellation of origin** are some of the best wines of Greece. Some 20 locations have been designated appellation of origin. In Northern Greece are the appellations Zitsa, Amyntaio, Goumenisa and Naousa. In Halkidiki is the appellation Playies Melitona. In Thessaly are the appellations Agialos and Rapsani. In the Athens area is the appellation of Kantza. In the Peloponnese are the appellations of Patras, Mantineia, and Nemea. In the Ionian islands is the appellations Rombola Cephalinias. In the islands of Paros, Limnos, Rhodes, and Santorini are the appellations (Paros, Limnos, Rhodes and Santorini). In Crete are the appellations of origin, Arkanes, Peza, Siteia and Daphnes.

Among the categories of local and table wines are pleasant, exhilarating flavours for lovers of wine.

INFORMATION

GENERAL INFORMATION

Greece is located in south-eastern Europe. Greece has a population of 10.964.020 (according to the census of 2001). Greece, a Presidential, Parliamentary Democracy, acceded to the European Union in 1981.

Athens is located in the Attica prefecture, in particular in the Attica basin, which is encompassed by Mount Aegaleo, Mount Parnitha, Mount Penteli and Mount Hymettos. Athens, the suburbs and the neighbouring town of Piraeus constitute an urban entity (greater urban complex of the capital) with a population of about 3.5 million residents.

CURRENCY: The national currency of Greece since January 1, 2001, is the **euro**. You can exchange currency at the airport, at private currency exchanges, and banks.

DIALLING CODE: The international dialling code of Greece is +30.

TIME ZONE: Athens time is seven hours ahead of Eastern Standard Time, two hours ahead of Greenwich Mean Time, and one hour ahead of Central European Time.

CLIMATE: Athens has a mild climate, with sunshine more than 260 days a year.

The average monthly temperature is:

Month	Temperature (in °C)
January	10,3
February	10,6
March	12,3
April	15,9
May	20,7
June	25,2
July	28,0
August	27,8
September	24,2
October	19,5
November	15,4
December	12,0

SEASONS

We recommend that you visit Athens any season. The tourist season is from April to October, peaking in August.

NATIONAL HOLIDAYS

New Year's Day: January 1st.

Epiphany: 6 January. Consecration of the waters in the Piraeus area. The Cross is cast in the sea and young men dive in to retrieve it.

Shrove Monday: 41 days before Easter. The commencement of Lenten fasting. On Shrove Monday Greeks fly kites, fast, and celebrate the Shrove Monday feast. Athenians enjoy a stroll at Philopappou Hill.

Independence Day and *the Annunciation:* 25 March. Military Parade.

Easter: Good Friday to Easter Bank Holiday. On Good Friday in the afternoon churches decorate an epitaph. The procession of the Epitaph is joined by people holding candles and singing psalms on the streets of every town and village in the country.

Resurrection: Celebrated with fireworks and flares at midnight, on the eve of Easter.

Easter Day: According to custom, on Easter Day, Greeks eat spited lamb. The festivities include music and dancing.

May Day: 1 May. A multitude of flower shows in Athens.

Pentecost: Celebrated 50 days after Easter.

The Dormition of the Virgin: On 15 August.

28 October: National holiday.

114

Military parade.

Christmas: 25-26 December.

OTHER TRADITIONAL HOLIDAYS:

Carnival: Carnival festivities of 3 weeks duration, ending on Shrove Monday. In Athens the main Carnival festivities are held in Plaka.

Wine Feast: Organised by a multitude of municipalities.

Nautical Week: Celebrated in Phaliron.

EMBASSIES - CONSULATES

For information regarding Embassies and Consulates, enquire at the Greek National Tourism Organisation or:

The Ministry of Foreign Affairs:
3, Akadimias Str (ground floor) information bureau
tel. 210 3682700, fax 210 3682474
e-mail: cio@mfa.gr
website: www.mfa.gr
opening hours 10:00-14:00

ABBREVIATIONS

You will come across a multitude of Greek abbreviations during your visit in Athens.

EOT: Greek National Tourism Organisation.

ELPA: Automobile and Touring Club of Greece.

ELTA: Hellenic Post Office.

KTEL: Inter-urban domestic buses.

OASA: Athens Urban Transport Organisation.

OSE: Hellenic Railways Organisation.

OTE: Hellenic Telecommunications Organisation.

ELECTRIC CURRENT

The standard electric current in Greece is 220V (50Hz) alternating current.

THE POST OFFICE

The signposts of post offices and post office boxes are usually bright yellow. Athens post offices are open from Monday to Friday from 07:30 to 14:00. Four post offices listed below have longer opening hours.

Mitropoleos Str, Syntagma Square.
tel. 210 3319500, 210 3237573, 210 3226253.
Open weekdays from 07:30 - 20:00
Saturdays from 07:30 - 14:00
Sundays from 09:00 - 13:00

100, Aeolou Str, Omonia Square.
tel. 210 3216024, 210 3253586
Opening hours on weekdays from 07:30 - 20:00
Saturdays from 07:30 - 14:00
Sundays from 09:00 - 13:00

Mitropoleos Square.
tel. 210 32 18 143
Opening hours weekdays
from 07:30 – 20:00
Saturdays 07:30 - 14:00
Closed on Sundays

Hellenic Post Office (EL.TA):
information tel. 800 1182000
website: www.elta-net.gr

Domestic-International Telegrams:
tel. 136

Post Office Phone Service:
tel. 800 1183000

Information regarding mail:
tel. 210 3216033

Door to Door Postal Service:
tel. 210 6073000

Parcels:
tel. 210 3473311 (domestic)
210 5249359 (international)

EMERGENCY NUMBERS

POLICE:

General Police Headquarters of Attica: 173, Alexandras Avenue, telephone 133; 210 6476000

Emergency number: tel. 100

Drugs Squad:
tel. 109; 210 6442913

115

Athens Traffic Police:
tel. 210 5284000

Piraeus Police Headquarters:
37, Iroon Polytechneiou Str.
tel. 210 4111710-9
210 4122501-5

Piraeus Traffic Police:
tel. 210 4177700

Airport police:
tel. 210 3536899

E.L.P.A.:
395, Mesogeion Avenue
tel. 210 6068800

E.L.P.A. Road Assistance:
tel. 10400

HEALTH CARE:

Emergency Number:
tel. 166

Emergency hospitals, pharmacies, doctors:
tel. 1434 (in Greek)

Medical information in Greek and English: tel. 210 8983146

Medical emergency help line:
tel. 210 7460000
210 7710621

SOS Doctors: tel. 1016

Blood donation centre:
tel. 210 8257425

Poisoning centre:
tel. 210 7793777

AIDS help line: tel. 210 7222222

Psychological emergency help line:
tel. 197

FIRE BRIGADE: tel. 199

TOURIST INFORMATION

GREEK NATIONAL TOURISM
ORGANISATION (E.O.T.):

Central Office:
7, Tsoha Str, 115 21 Athens
tel. 210 8707000
e-mail: info@gnto.gr
website: www.gnto.gr

Athens information centre: 26 A,
Amalias Str, Syntagma - Athens

tel. 210 3310392, 210 3310716,
210 3310640

"Eleftherios Venizelos" airport information centre:
tel. 210 3530445-448
e-mail: venizelos@gnto.gr

Greek National Tourism Organisation Offices Abroad:
For Greek National Tourism
Organisation Offices enquire at the
Organisation's central office or visit
the web page www.gnto.gr/1/01/
0113/ea0113001.html

TOURIST POLICE:
A department of the Greek Police
(EL.AS), manned by specially
trained men and women, providing
information and assistance to
tourists. The Tourist Police are
authorised to settle minor disputes
between tourists and tourist
businesses. Tourist Police speak
foreign languages. Officers wear the
insignia "Tourist Police" on the
shoulder. For tourist information
dial **171** any time and day, at any
location in the country.

Athens Tourist Police Station:
43, Veikou Str, Koukaki
tel. 210 9200724-27

Piraeus Tourist Police Station:
Xaveriou Str, tel. 210 4290664-5

HOTELS

In Athens and the greater Athens
area (including the suburbs, Piraeus,
and Attica), are more than 700
lodgings of all categories, with a
total capacity of about 62,000 beds.
Most of the lodgings have been
renovated and modernised recently
and have high quality, modern
facilities.

The Hotel Chamber of Greece:
24, Stadiou Str, 105 64 Athens
tel. 210 3310022-6
for reservations dial 210 32 37 193
fax 210 3225449
e-mail: grhotels@otenet.gr

The Hellenic Hoteliers Association (P.O.X.):
24, Stadiou Str, 105 64 Athens

116

tel 210 3312535-6
fax 210 3230636
e-mail: pox@otenet.gr
website: www.pox.gr

The Hellenic Union of Campsite Owners:
102, Solonos Str, 106 73 Athens
tel. 210 3621560, 210 5222723
fax 210 3621560, opening hours:
Monday to Thursday 6-9 pm.

The Hellenic Youth Hostels Union:
11, Botasi Str, tel. 210 3837449
fax 210 3235790

The Greek Youth Hostel Organisation: 75, Damareos Str.
tel. 210 7519530

TOURIST ORGANISATIONS

ORGANISED TOURS-EXCURSIONS:
For organised tours of Athens, the Attica area, the islands of the Saronic Gulf, and other areas of Greece (among others, Delphi, Mykines, Epidavros, Meteora, Northern Greece) contact the Greek National Tourism Organisation or:

The Hellenic Tourist and Travel Agents Association:
11, Iosif Rogon Str, 117 42 Athens
tel. 210 9223522, 210 9234143
fax 210 9233307
e-mail: hatta@hatta.gr
website: www.hatta.gr

CAR RENTAL: In the Athens area are many reliable car rental companies, most of them located at Syngrou Avenue. For information regarding car rentals contact:

Hellenic Car Rental Association:
576, Vouliagmenis Avenue,
Agryroupoli, tel. 210 9942850-9

YACHT BROKERS:
Yacht brokers. For yacht rentals contact the following organisations:

Hellenic Yacht Brokers and Consultants Association:

Office A1 in Zea Marina, 185 36
Piraeus; tel. 210 4533134
fax 210 4533134
e-mail: hyba@ath.forthnet.gr

The Hellenic Professional Yacht Owners Association:
A8 Zea Marina, 185 36 Piraeus
tel. 210 4280465, 210 4526335

BEACHES

In the southern suburbs of Athens, along the Saronic Gulf (from the P. Faliro area to Vouliagmeni), and other areas of Attica, are dozens of organised and other beaches, with clean waters and easy access. Several Attica beaches have been awarded **"Blue Flags of Europe"**, granted every year to beaches and marines meeting strict criteria regarding clean waters and beaches, good organisation and security and the protection of the coastal environment. For the programme visit the website:
www.blueflag.org/Map_Greece.asp#

ORGANISED BEACHES (with entry ticket):
Grand Beach Lagonissi, Asteria Seaside, Asteras Vouliagmenis Plage, Vouliagmenis Lake, Attica Vouliagmenis Beach, Voula Beach A', Varkiza Beach, Ayiou Kosma Beach, Voula Beach B', Alimos.

OTHER BEACHES:

Southern Attica: Vouliagmeni – Deftero Limanaki; Anavyssos – Eden and Thymari; Sounio (KAPE, Legraina, Temple of Poseidon, Sounio-Poseidonia Coast), Patroclos Island.

Eastern Attica: Kerateas beach (Kakia Thalassa), Porto Rafti (Avlaki-Ayia Marina, Erotospilia), Vravrona-Artemis (Hamolia, Aghiou Nikolaou Artemidos Beach); Rafina (Marikes Plage, Kokkino Limanaki); Nea Makri (Zoumberi, Mati, Paralia Neas Makris); Marathon (Schinias - Karavi,

Dikastika, Ramnountas, Sesi).

Northern Attica: Oropos (Ayioi Apostoloi, Paralia Kalamou, Oropos-Nea Palatia, Pigadakia Halkoutsiou).

Western Attica: Porto Germeno, Psatha, Strava.

MARINAS

In Attica are 6 marinas, with a total capacity of about 3,000 boats.

Alimos marina:
tel/fax 210 9821850, 210 9828642

Floisvos marina:
tel/fax 210 9829218

Glyfada marina:
tel/fax 210 8947353, 210 8947374

Vouliagmenis marina:
tel/fax 210 8960012-4

Zeas Piraeus marina:
tel/fax 210 4513623, 210 4184182

Lavrion Olympic marina:
tel. 22920 63700
For further information regarding marinas contact the Greek National Tourism Organisation or

Tourist Property Association (E.T.A.):
7, Voulis Str, 105 62 Athens
tel. 210 3339513, 210 3339416
fax 210 3339500
e-mail: info@etasa.gr
website: www.etasa.gr

PUBLIC TRANSPORT

URBAN BUS LINES:
For information on bus lines call tel. 185 (in Greek);
website www.oasa.gr

ATHENS METRO:
At every stop you can find a table with all the lines and routes of the metro trains.
Website: www.ametro.gr

ATHENS TRAM:
website: www.tramsa.gr

ATHENS INTERNATIONAL AIRPORT "Eleftherios Venizelos":
190 19 Spata , Greece;

tel. 210 3530000, fax 210 3530001, website www.aia.gr
Bus lines linking the airport to the greater Athens urban complex: number E95 (to Syntagma, Athens), E96 (to Piraeus), E92 (to Kifissia), E93 (to the inter-city bus terminal), E94 (to metro stop "Ethniki Amyna") and E97 (to metro stop "Dafni"). Moreover the Suburban Railway and the metro links the airport to Athens.

Olympic Airlines:
Information - reservations
tel. 210 9666666, 801 11 44444
website: www.olympic-airways.gr

Aegean Airlines:
information- reservations
tel. 210 9988300, 801 11 20000
website: www.aegeanair.gr

HELLENIC RAILWAYS ORGANISATION (O.S.E.):
1-3, Karolou Str, information on domestic and international train schedules: tel. 210 5297777; 140
website: www.ose.gr

SEA TRANSPORT:

Information on schedules:
tel 1440

Central Pireaus Harbour Police:
tel. 210 4226000-4

Saronic Gulf Lines (Piraeus):
tel. 210 4124585

Rafina Harbour Police:
tel. 22940 22300

Lavrion Harbour Police:
tel. 22920 25249

INTERCITY BUS STATIONS:
Buses for all regions and Attica depart from three bus stations. (information tel.1440
website: www.ktel.org)

1st Station: 100, Kifissou Str.
tel. 210 5124910-11-14

2nd Station: 260, Liosion Str.
tel. 210 8317179

Athens prefecture KTEL:
tel. 210 8230179 (Sounio, Oropos, Porto Rafti, Markopoulo)
210 8210872 (Marathon)

TAXI:
All taxis have a taxi counter, recording charges. Drivers are obliged to set the counter at every fare. From 05:00 - 24:00 hours tariff 1 is used and from 24:00 - 05:00 tariff 2. Taxis are supplied with a valid price list, recording the fare and surplus charges not recorded by the taximeter.

MUSEUMS

In Athens, Piraeus, the suburbs, and environs, are a multitude of important museums. The list below includes a selection of museums. For information regarding museums, visit the site www.culture.gr.

The National Archaeological Museum: 144, Patision Str.
tel. 210 8217717, 210 8217724

The Acropolis Museum (in the archaeological area):
tel. 210 3236665, 210 3210219

The Athens Ancient Agora Museum:
Stoa tou Attalou, Archaea Agora;
tel. 210 3210185

The Kerameikos Museum:
148, Ermou Str, tel. 210 3463552

The Epigraph Museum:
1, Tositsa Str, tel. 210 8217637

The Numismatic Museum:
12, Panepistimiou Str ("Iliou Melathron")
tel. 210 3643774, 210 3612540
website: www.nm.culture.gr

The Goulandris Museum of Cycladic and Ancient Greek Art:
4, Neofytou Douka Str.
tel. 210 7226321-3
website: www.cycladic-m.gr

The Acropolis Research Centre:
2-4, Makriyianni Str.
tel. 210 9239381

The National Historical and Ethnological Museum:
13, Stadiou Str, tel. 210 3237617

The Benaki Museum: 1, Koumbari Str. & Vas. Sofias Avenue
tel. 210 3671000

website: www.benaki.gr
- *Piraeus Street building:*
138, Pireaus Str. (Gazi)
tel. 210 3453111

The Byzantine and Christian Museum: 22, Vas. Sofias Avenue,
tel. 210 7211027, 210 7232178

The War Museum:
2, Rizari Str, tel. 210 7252974-6

The Museum of the City of Athens:
5-7, Paparrigopoulou Str.
(Klafthmonos Square)
tel. 210 3246164
website: www.athenscitymuseum.gr

The National Gallery-Alexandros Soutzos Museum:
50, Vas. Konstantinou Avenue
tel. 210 7235857

The National Museum of Modern Art: Syngrou Avenue, FIX building;
tel. 210 9242111-2

The Athens Municipal Gallery:
51, Piraeus Str, Koumoundourou Square
tel. 210 2231841, 210 3240472

The Frissiras Museum:
3-7, Monis Asteriou Str, Plaka
tel. 210 3234678
website: www.frissirasmuseum.com

The Greek Popular Art Museum:
17, Kythathinaeon Str, Plaka
tel. 210 3229031, 210 3213018

The Greek Traditional Musical Instruments Museum:
1-3, Diogenous Str, Plaka
tel. 210 3250198
     210 3254119-129

The Ceramics Collection:
Tzistaraki Mosque, Monastiraki
tel. 210 3242006

The Hellenic Children's Museum:
14, Kythatinaeon Str.
tel. 210 3312995-6
website: www.hcm.gr

The Historical Museum of the University of Athens: 5, Tholou Str, Plaka, tel. 210 3240861

The Kanellopoulos Museum:
12, Theorias Str & Panos Str, Plaka
tel. 210 3212313

The Theatrical Museum:
50, Akadimias Str, tel. 210 3629430

119

The Eleftherios Venizelos Museum: Eleftherias Square, tel. 210 7224238

The Eleftherias Square Art Centre: 10, Evzonon Str, tel. 210 7232603

The Newer Ceramics Research Centre: 4-5, Melidoni Str, Kerameikos tel. 210 3318491-6

The Ilias Lalaounis Jewellery Museum: 12, Kalisperi Str, Acropolis; tel. 210 9221044

The Maria Callas Museum ("Technopolis"): 100, Piraeus Str, Gazi, tel. 210 3467322

The Jewish Museum: 29, Nikis Str, tel. 210 3225582

The Foundation of the Hellenic World : 18, Poulopoulou Str, Theseion, tel. 210 3422292
- *Cultural Centre:* 254, Piraeus, Tavros, Athens, tel. 210 4835300 website: www.ime.gr

The Goulandri Museum of Natural History: 13, Levidou Str, Kifissia, tel. 210 8015870 website: www.gnhm.gr
- *"Gaia" Centre:* 100, Othonos Str.

The Vorres Museum: 1, Parodos Diadohou Konstantinou Str, Paiania tel. 210 6642520, 210 6644771

The Piraeus Archaeological Museum: 31, Harilaou Trikoupi Str. tel. 210 4521598

The Piraeus Nautical Museum: Themistocleous Str, Piraeus tel. 210 4286959, 210 4516264

Sounio Archaeological site: tel. 22920 39363

Elefsina Archaeological site (Museum): tel. 210 55 46 019

The Marathon Archaeological Museum: 114, Plataion Str, Marathon; tel. 22940 55 155

The Tomb of Marathon: tel. 22950 55462

Ramnounda Archaeological site: tel. 22940 63477

Amphiaraeio Archaeological site: tel. 22950 61144

Vravron Archaeological site: tel. 22990 27020

CULTURAL EVENTS

For cultural events in Athens see foreign language newspapers on sale at central kiosks (among others, Syntagma Square, Omonia Square), or website: www.cultureguide.gr

ATHENS FESTIVAL:
The Athens Festival, established in 1955, is held in summer (June - September) at the open air Roman Herodus Atticus Odeon. It is one of Europe's major festivals. Some of the best Greek and foreign groups and artists perform classical and modern music, opera, dance and theatre. The Festival in summer holds important cultural events at the Lykavittos theatre.

Hellenic Festival S.A.: Makriyianni Str and 23, Hadjichristou Str, 117 42 Athens; information and reservations tel. 210 9282900 fax 210 9292933 e-mail: press@greekfestival.gr website: www.hellenicfestival.gr

Central ticket office: 39, Panepistimiou Str. (in the arcade); tel. 210 3221459; opening hours: 08:30 – 16:00 (Monday to Friday) 09:00 – 14:30 (Saturdays)

The Odeion of Herodes Atticus ticket office: tel. 210 32 32 771 opening hours: 09:00 – 14:00 & 18:00 – 21:00

Lykavittos theatre ticket office: tel. 210 7227233, 210 7227209

THE ATHENS CONCERT HALL:
Vas. Sofias Str. & Kokkali Str, 115 21 Athens; information - reservations tel. 210 7282333 e-mail: webmaster@megaron.gr website: www.megaron.gr

Central ticket office: opening hours: Monday - Friday 10:00 - 16:00; Saturday 10:00 -14:00 and 18:00 - 20:30; Sunday 18:00 - 20:30

Ticket office in the city centre:

Omirou Str 8, opening hours
Monday – Friday 10:00 – 16:00

THE NATIONAL OPERA HOUSE:

The oldest opera theatre in Greece. Opera and ballet performances and music concerts are held in its two auditoria, ("Olympia" and "Acropol" theatre) (website: www.nationalopera.gr)

The "Olympia" Theatre: 59, Akadimias Str, 106 79 Athens, information - reservations tel. 210 3612461, 210 3643725 fax 210 3612461

The "Acropol" Theatre: 9-11, Ippokratous Str, 106 79 Athens; information - reservations tel. 210 3643700, 210 3608666 fax 210 3609003

LYKEION TON IHELLINIDON (Lyceum Club of Greek Women):

Founded in 1910 by the first Greek feminist K. Paren, the Lykeion ton Hellinidon seeks to preserve Greek folk custom, research and study different varieties of Greek national dress, record Greek folk music, and study and perform Greek folk dances. The Lyceum's museum exhibits a valuable collection of genuine Greek dresses from every part of the country. Members of the Lyceum's folk dance group wear valuable dresses during performances in Greece and abroad (14, Dimokritou Str, Kolonaki; tel. 210 3639704).

DORA STRATOU THEATRE:

(● page 41), tel. 210 3244395, 210 9214650, fax 210 3246921

ATHENS MUNICIPALITY CULTURAL ORGANISATION:

stages cultural and sporting events. Information: tel. 210 3621601, 210 3630706, fax 210 3614358 e-mail: mail@athens-culture.gr website: www.athens-culture.gr

OPEN AIR CINEMAS:

rank among Greece's attractions. Athenians in summer evenings like to see a movie in a garden with trees and flowers, beneath a starlit sky. In Greece films are not dubbed. Foreign films have Greek subtitles.

SPORT

The Culture Ministry – Sub-Ministry of Sport: 7, Kifissias Avenue, 115 23 Athens tel. 210 6496000 website: www.sportsnet.gr.

The Sports Federations: website: www.sportsnet.gr/3/e31.html

The Hellenic Olympic Committee (E.O.E.): 52, Dim Vikela Str. (372, Kifissias Avenue) 152 33 Halandri, Athens tel. 210 6878809, 210 68 78 888 fax 210 6878840 website: www.hoc.gr

The "Athens 2004" Olympic Games Organising Committee: 8, Iolkou Str. & Filikis Etairias, 142 34 N. Ionia (Athens) tel. 210 2004000; fax 210 2004004 e-mail: welcome@athens2004.com website: www.athens2004.com

WEBSITES

ATHENS MUNICIPALITY:
www.cityofathens.gr

MINISTRY OF CULTURE:
Information on archaeological sites and historical monuments www.culture.gr

MODERN ARCHITECTURE in ATHENS - ATTICA:
www.culture2000.tee.gr

UNIFICATION OF THE ARCHAEOLOGICAL SITES OF ATHENS:
www.astynet.gr

ATHENS NEWS AGENCY:
www.ana.gr

USEFUL INFORMATION

⊠	Post Office (EL.TA.)	⎙	Telecommunications (O.T.E.)
⊕	State Hospital	🏀	Basket Ball
▣	Tennis Court	▨	Pedestrians Road
🏐	Volley Ball	E95	Bus to the Airport

122

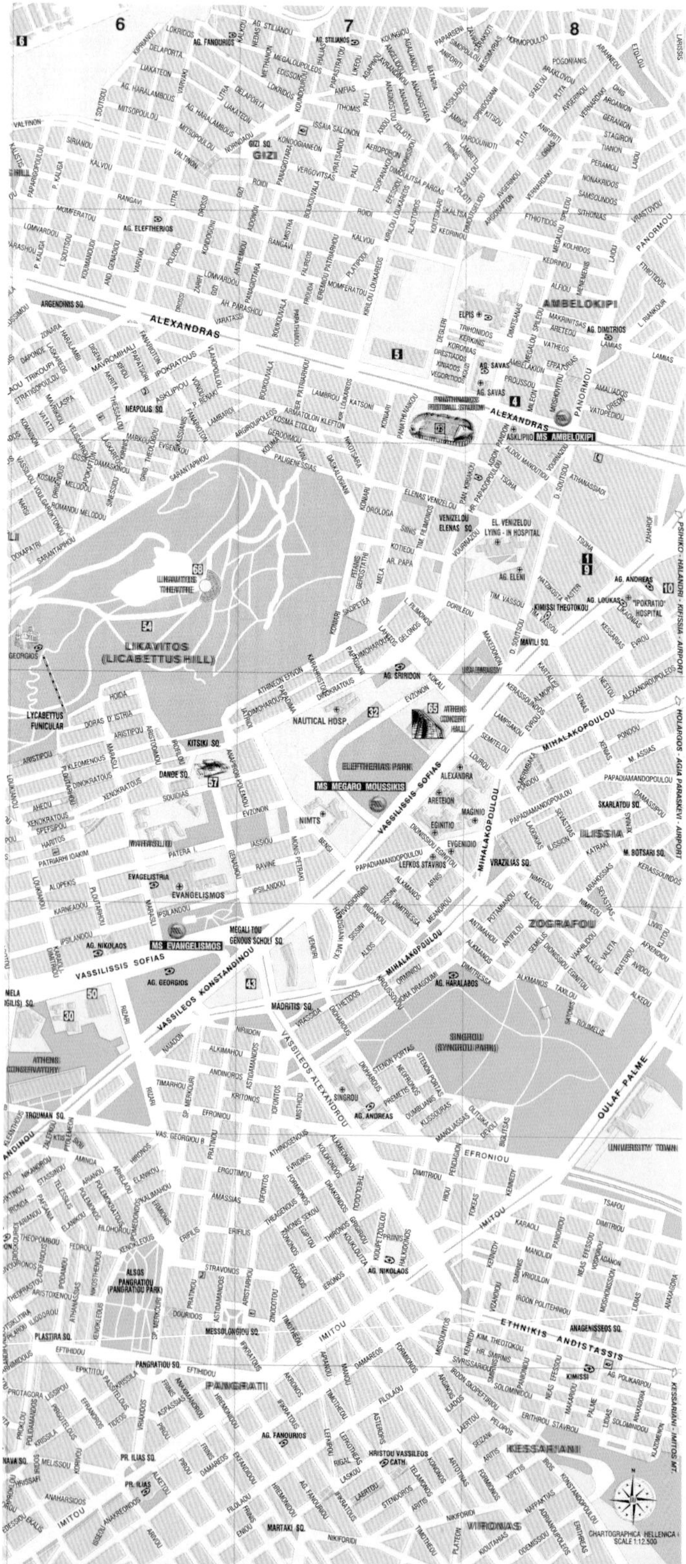
6
7
8
GIZI
AMBELOKIPI
ALEXANDRAS
LIKAVITOS (LICABETTUS HILL)
LYCABETTUS FUNICULAR
NAUTICAL HOSP.
ATHENS CONCERT HALL
ELEFTHERIAS PARK
MS MEGARO MOUSSIKIS
MS AMBELOKIPI
MS EVANGELISMOS
VASSILISSIS SOFIAS
VASSILEOS KONSTANDINOU
VASSILEOS ALEXANDROU
MIHALAKOPOULOU
EVANGELISMOS
ZOGRAFOU
ILISSIA
SINGROU (SYNGROU PARK)
OULAF PALME
UNIVERSITY TOWN
ATHENS CONSERVATORY
TRUMAN SQ.
ALSOS PANGRATIOU (PANGRATIOU PARK)
PANGRATI
IMITOU
ETHNIKIS ANDISTASSIS
KESSARIANI
VIRONAS
PLASTIRA SQ.
PANGRATIOU SQ.
MESSOLONGIOU SQ.
MADRITIS SQ.
KITSIKI SQ.
DEXE SQ.
MAVILI SQ.
"IPOKRATIO" HOSPITAL
EL. VENIZELOU LYING - IN HOSPITAL
PSIHIKO - HALANDRI - KIFISSIA - AIRPORT
HOLARGOS - AGIA PARASKEVI - AIRPORT
KESSARIANI - IMITOS MT.
CHARTOGRAPHICA HELLENICA
SCALE 1:12.500

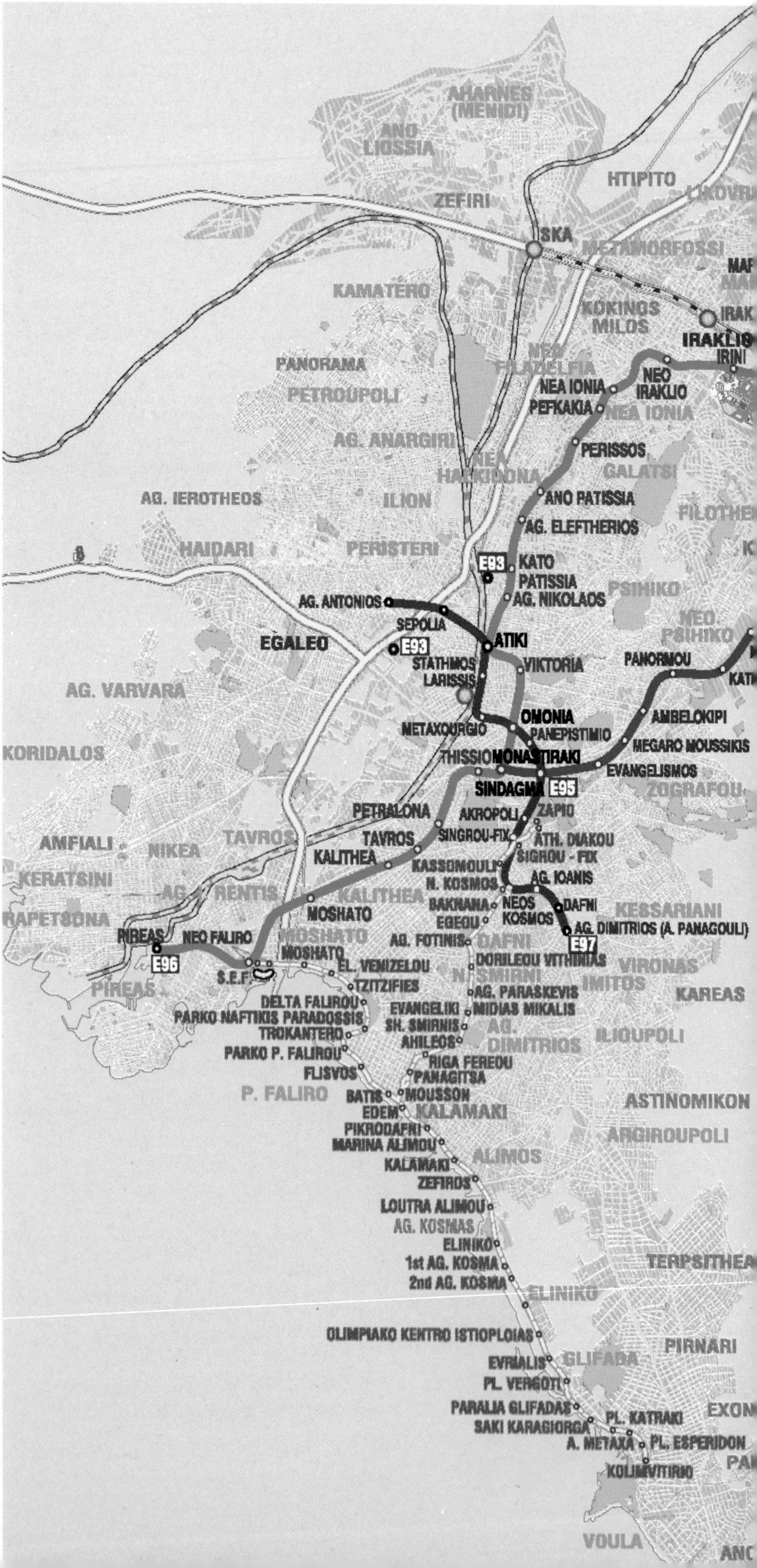
AHARNES (MENIDI)
ANO LIOSSIA
ZEFIRI
SKA
HTIPITO
METAMORFOSSI
KAMATERO
KOKINOS MILOS
IRAKLIO
PANORAMA
PETROUPOLI
NEA FILADELFIA
NEA IONIA
NEO IRAKLIO
IRINI
PEFKAKIA
PERISSOS
GALATSI
AG. ANARGIRI
NEA HALKIDONA
ANO PATISSIA
AG. IEROTHEOS
ILION
AG. ELEFTHERIOS
HAIDARI
PERISTERI
KATO PATISSIA
AG. NIKOLAOS
PSIHIKO
NEO PSIHIKO
AG. ANTONIOS
SEPOLIA
ATIKI
EGALEO
PANORMOU
VIKTORIA
STATHMOS LARISSIS
AG. VARVARA
AMBELOKIPI
OMONIA
METAXOURGIO
PANEPISTIMIO
MEGARO MOUSSIKIS
KORIDALOS
THISSIO
MONASTIRAKI
EVANGELISMOS
SINDAGMA
ZOGRAFOU
PETRALONA
AKROPOLI
ZAPIO
AMFIALI
TAVROS
SINGROU-FIX
ATH. DIAKOU
NIKEA
KALITHEA
SIGROU - FIX
KERATSINI
KASSOMOULIS
AG. IOANIS
RENTIS
N. KOSMOS
DAFNI
DRAPETSONA
BAKRANA
NEOS KOSMOS
KESSARIANI
MOSHATO
EGEOU
AG. DIMITRIOS (A. PANAGOULI)
PIREAS
NEO FALIRO
AG. FOTINIS
DAFNI
MOSHATO
EL. VENIZELOU
DORILEOU VITHINIAS
VIRONAS
S.E.F.
TZITZIFIES
N. SMIRNI
IMITOS
PIREAS
AG. PARASKEVIS
KAREAS
DELTA FALIROU
EVANGELIKI
MIDIAS MIKALIS
PARKO NAFTIKIS PARADOSSIS
TROKANTERO
SH. SMIRNIS
AG. DIMITRIOS
ILIOUPOLI
AHILEOS
PARKO P. FALIROU
RIGA FEREOU
FLISVOS
PANAGITSA
P. FALIRO
BATIS
MOUSSON
EDEM
KALAMAKI
ASTINOMIKON
PIKRODAFNI
MARINA ALIMOU
ARGIROUPOLI
KALAMAKI
ALIMOS
ZEFIROS
LOUTRA ALIMOU
AG. KOSMAS
ELINIKO
1st AG. KOSMA
TERPSITHEA
2nd AG. KOSMA
ELINIKO
OLIMPIAKO KENTRO ISTIOPLOIAS
PIRNARI
EVRIALIS
GLIFADA
PL. VERGOTI
PARALIA GLIFADAS
PL. KATRAKI
SAKI KARAGIORGA
A. METAXA
PL. ESPERIDON
KOLIMVITIRIO
VOULA
E93
E95
E96
E97

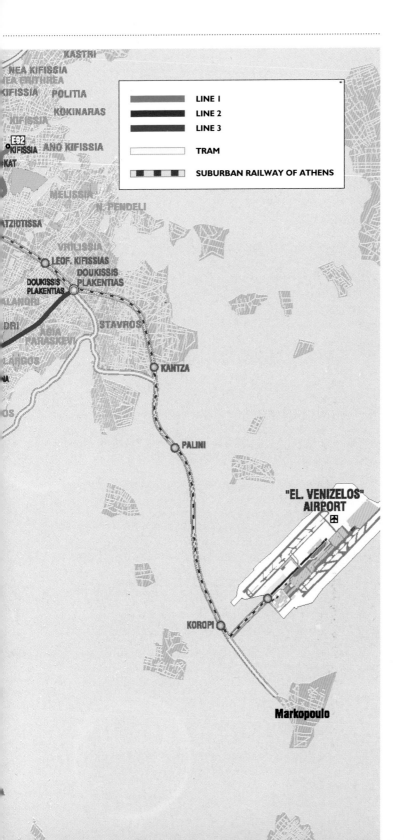

MINISTRY OF TOURISM
PUBLICATION OF THE GREEK NATIONAL TOURISM ORGANISATION
No 19 – JULY 2004

Publication Supervision: IRINI FRANGIADAKI
Director of the Directorate
of Market Research and Advertising

Publication Co-ordinator: LOUISA STAVROPOULOU-BRIOLA
Head of the Department of Publications
and Audiovisual Media

Research - Concept - Texts: GIANNIS RAGKOS

Translation: ALEXI PAPASOTIRIOU

Lay Out: M&M ADVERTISING

Photographs: GNTO ARCHIVE, A' DEPARTMENT OF
PRE-HISTORIC AND CLASSICAL ANTIQUITIES, C' DEPARTMENT
OF PRE-HISTORIC AND CLASSICAL ANTIQUITIES,
ARCHAEOLOGICAL RESOURCES FUND, BENAKI MUSEUM
ARCHIVE, K. VERGAS, Y. YIANNELOS, G. GRIGORIOU,
A. DROUGAS, N. KONTOS, M. MITZITHROPOULOS,
A. SMARAGDIS, P. STOLIS, K. TSIGANOS, PHOTOKINISI,
Ch. CHRISTODOULIDIS, E. HOLAN.

- We thank the General Director of the Ministry of Culture
for the provision of photographic material.

Drawings: A' DEPARTMENT OF PRE-HISTORIC AND CLASSICAL
ANTIQUITIES, Y. TRAVLOS, M. KORRES

Management: ANTONIS CHRISTIDIS

Maps: CHARTOGRAPHICA HELLENICA

Printed by: G. DETORAKIS S.A.

ISBN: 960 - 534 - 036 - 4

GREEK NATIONAL TOURISM ORGANISATION
www.gnto.gr

128